QUINTESSENCE

QUINTESSENCE

QUINTESSENCE

William F. DeVault

QUINTESSENCE

©2019 Venetian Spider Press™
All rights reserved.
ISBN: 1-7326794-9-8
ISBN-13: 978-1-7326794-9-8

QUINTESSENCE

To all the totem-muses who have stayed in my graces:
Alabaster, Psyche, Valkyrie, the Mad Gypsy, the Butterfly, Suede,
Goldenheart, Agnia, Lola, Nightblooming Jasmine,
Pink Champagne, Looking Glass, the Truth, and Padparadscha.
May you all, one day, embrace your immortality with joy and peace.
You are all part of this volume and I am grateful for your existence and patience.

Contents

A VERY BRIEF INTRODUCTION 1

FROM THE BOOK GRACE. 2

    Grace 3
    The Merchant, The Priest, and The Poet 4
    Inkwell 5
    watch the horizon for signs of life 6
    Two Feet of Snow in Buffalo 7
    Impaired 8
    Dragons do not rise, the ground falls away 9
    Patchwork Hearts 9
    Seduction in G sharp 10
    Legends of songs in a cave 11
    Flying Elves 11
    Trippingly 12
    Visions without Eyes 12
    Lola Montez 13
    I will find you 13
    legacy 14
    shadows and smoke 14
    in the erotique... 15
    linotte: a contemplation 15
    Disease 16
    Sinister and Sweet 17
    Public 18
    expressions 19
    I linger at the well 20
    real woman 21
    In the Heat of the Moment 22
    Feasting on a Lover 22
    Menu 23
    A Deep and Resonant Purr.. 23
    Constant Seductions 24
    Midnight Musing 24
    Immortal 25
    Negotiation 25
    Pale Minstrel 26
    Snowflakes are Imperfect 27
    Centigrade 27
    Banquet of the Vanquished 28
    My Fine Fae Lady 29
    Not a dream passes 30
    Once again 31
    Flash and Fire 32
    Driftwood 32
    The Sonnets of Grace: I 33
    The Sonnets of Grace: II 33
    The Sonnets of Grace: III 34
    The Sonnets of Grace: IIII 34
    The Sonnets of Grace: V 35

THE SONNETS OF GRACE: VI	35
THE SONNETS OF GRACE: VII	36
THE SONNETS OF GRACE: VIII	36
THE SONNETS OF GRACE: VIIII	37
THE SONNETS OF GRACE: X	37
THE SONNETS OF GRACE: XI	38
THE SONNETS OF GRACE: XII	38
THE SONNETS OF GRACE: XIII	39
THE SONNETS OF GRACE: XIIII	39
THE SONNETS OF GRACE: DIADEM	40

FROM THE BOOK CLEAVE (COMING TOGETHER): ... 41

STRANGE…BUT BEAUTIFUL	42
BASE SACRAMENTS	43
I STAND FOR YOU	44
THIN SKIN	44
THE SATYR'S SUIT	45
GENII	46
ASIDE, ASTRIDE THE PHOENIX	47
BEHIND THE FAÇADE	48
THE PRIEST OF PASSION SERVES THE SACRAMENT	49
THE GODDESS WALKS	50
CENTAUR	51
AUBERGINE CONFESSION	52
DANCE NAKED IN THE SKY (FOR THE RIGHT SET OF LIPS)	53
FAERIE: LOVE	54
IN THE STRANGEST CORNERS OF MEMORY	55
KISS ME	56
I FIND	57
THUNDER OF LUST	58
YIELDING TO TEMPTATION	59
MY PASSION, MY CATHEDRAL	60
YOU ARE A CHARITY TO THIS SPHERE	61
THE PLUCK OF PAN	62
ABDICATION	63
THE FORGE OF APHRODITE	64
PARAMOUR AND NOTHING MORE	64
I WILL PASS THROUGH THE FIRE	66
HEPHAESTUS TO APHRODITE	67
ANGELS SLEEP	68
BRISANT REVELATIONS	69
CLOSE YOUR EYES	70
TIP FOR TAP	71
DARE WE CROSS THE RUBICON?	72
HOW WOULD YOU HAVE ME TOUCH YOU?	73
JASMINE AND PLUMERIA	74
THE PHILOSOPHY OF DREAMS	75
DAMASCUS, MOVEMENT 7	76
WINE	77
DRAM	77
DAMASCUS, MOVEMENT 3	78
SPARKS, LIKE FROZEN LEMONS	79
IN THE ARMS OF THE DRAGON	80

A Summoned Fire	81
Monument	81
The Unicorns	82
The Faceted Sphere: One	82

FROM THE BOOK CLEAVE (SPLITTING APART) 83

Nemicorn	83
My Electric Lady	84
The Reich of Self-discipline	85
The Common Tongue	86
Will You Be with Me Tonight?	86
Votive	87
The Frost of Ill-remembranced Things	88
The Taste of Remembrance	89
The Patchwork Skirt of My Love	90
TRANSCENDENCE	91
Into the Grey	92
In the Morning I Will Be Gone	93
I Will Come for Tea	94
From the Parapet	95
Love is an Howling Beast	96
Sisyphus and Prometheus	97
Threnody for Times Now Past: 3/17/1979	98
A Vile Attar	99
More Than Flesh	100
Waiting for the Pentecost	101
Shroud	102
The Bottom of the Bottle	103
Final Sunday	104
Bohemia	105

FROM THE BOOK MYTHOS: 106

Prologue	107
Woo	108
the madness of the elvish goddess	108
fusion	109
dread nemicorn	109
arrogant tongue	109
sultry summer afternoon	110
on the edge of night	110
ethereal eroticism	111
Desire, dire and sacred	111
petals touch	112
Diving Deep	112
demarcation (pause)	113
lightning and thunder	114
pride and perfect kisses	114
Persephone	114
Xochiquetzal	115
Holle	116
Venus	117
Bast	117
Qetesh	118

SAGA	118
ATTAR OF THE ALTAR	118
SIN	119
AMOMANCIES	119
LIP SERVICE	120
SHALL I STAND IN THE SHADOWS	120
TO SERVE THE COURTESAN	121
SHARED SACRAMENT	122
VECTOR	122
SOLFERINO SYMPHONIES	123
FLOW	124
TO SPEAK OF LOVE IN MANY WAYS	124
COMPATIBILITY	125
ARTIST	125
WHERE I KISS YOU IS A SACRAMENT	126

FROM THE BOOK **BRAGI** 127

BRAGI BLEEDS	128
PIG IRON AND THE MYTH OF IDOLATRY	128
ECLIPSE IN OLYMPUS	128
INFIDELITY	130
TOTEMIC	130
THE GRIEF OF BRAGI AND APOLLO	131
RIGHT THERE	132
EVOLUTION	132
WE ARE SOCIAL CREATURES	133
DJINN	133
BRAGI TO FREYA, ON HIS DEATHBED	134
BONFIRE	136
AND A DOVE	136
LEARNING OF THE DEATH OF A WELL-REGARDED EX-LOVER	137
FEIGNING	137
EVIL	138
THE MOMENT	138
BORDERS	139
CHASING APOLLO	139
RAKU: 1	140
RAKU: 2	140
RAKU: 3	141
RAKU: 4	141
RAKU: 5	141
RAKU: 6	142
RAKU: 7	142
PYEWACKET	143
I DO NOT CHASE THE WIND	144
WALSINGHAM IN PADUA	145
IN THE HALL OF MIRRORS: TWENTY	146
ERATO BEATS HER CHILDREN	147
THE RISE OF BRAGI	148
ROMANTIQUE	148
SIGYN FOR MY SINS	149
BRUTUS: ACT ONE	150
HEPHAESTUS TO APHRODITE	151

APHRODITE	152
ATHENA	152
HERA	152
ARTEMIS	152
DEMETER	153
DIONYSIA	153
THE MUSES	153
WHAT REMAINS OF THE STREET	154
FEEDING THE WOLF	155
HETAERON	156
WHEN THE MORNING NEVER COMES	156
COLLISION WITH THE MORNING STAR	157
MIDNIGHT AND THE HEAT RISES	158
I AM THE SERPENT	159
MORAL SENTIENCE	159
LITTLE SECRETS	160
THE SABOTAGE OF GODS	161
FALLING INTO DARKNESS	162
DFW	163
QOHELETH	164
ANTIQUATED	165
BEYOND ME	166
CONTEMPLATIVE SEDUCTION	167
SURREALITY	167
WHAT DARK MAGICKS	168
THE BLOOD OF KVASIR	168
ABOUT THE AUTHOR	171
ACKNOWLEDGEMENTS	171

A very brief introduction

If you happen to own one or more of the constituent volumes merged herein, don't feel bad.

They (**Grace**, **Cleave**, **Mythos**, **Bragi**) stand alone on their own, certainly.

But…when merged with the other three sisters of this set, they create a more intense and vivid landscape and portrait of my works during the four-year period in which they were published. Inspired by specific moment and muses, they are a collection of verbal photographs and I would not change a thing about them. I wrestled with having this volume in some order other than by original volume and poem order but decided this would tamper with the flow and content of the original. These were issued approximately 12 months apart over a period in my life where I surrendered to the flow of emotions and passions, while funneling, channeling, the intensity to the page.

To you unfamiliar with my works and particularly with the totem-muses that have driven them, relax and enjoy. You will find, no matter what you are comfortable with or seek for, poems within this collection that will satisfy you and your needs.

The decision to bring all four of these books, including two of my best-selling collections, into a single volume was a logical extension of my desire to make books that are durable. The market is aflood with the new generation chapbooks, a sometimes unfortunate by-product of the digital renaissance, but I have always liked the feel of a solid, substantial volume in my hands. The fact that we are co-issuing this in hardback, softcover, and eBook formats is a nod to the reality of the marketplace and the diversity of the readers, wanting to satisfy all interested in diving in.

Enjoy, and don't hesitate to reach out with any questions or comments. I don't hide.

William F. DeVault
November 2019

from the book **Grace.**

Cover of and by Aysha Nasser, 2014

Grace

release the troubled memories that hold you in their bonds,
liberation for our pain and stain for what our merge responds.
grace. a trace of sweetness. musky, like dusk, jasmine and saffron.
the thermodynamics of an ancient, urgent heat, action and reaction
as the parabola of kisses misses nothing worth mention, intention
sown and reaped, moistures seep and weep and keep the tension
barely bearable. I communicate a wordless poetry in surrender,
tender as a sacrifice to a price for bartered beauty, defender
of that which has already been given in chaste clarity and charity,
a gift to the magi who imagined us as spirits of inescapable verity.
hold nothing back not even the blackness and I will not slack
in my prescient tense of what you desire and require, no lack
of ardour and all my amomancies have become apprenticings
to your escape from the grey to lay claim to all your whims and wings.

The Merchant, The Priest, and The Poet

more than words.
the magic. tragic hopes.
the moments we barter.
merchants in the temple
where the priest sadly
shakes his head.
the barter economy
of love and passion.
copper for silver.
silver for gold.
gold for blood and fire.
desire.
ancient runes.
ancient tunes.
translated with light
that dances
barefoot.
the soft pad of feet
on cool stone
when the warm bed
makes a fine altar
for sacrifices.
the clarity of charity
in the ecclesiastical sense
where love requires
nothing.
but hopes for
everything.

Inkwell

I will write a sonnet
(perhaps even a villanelle)
in living fluid on the flesh of your naked form.
Hoping my words enter you.
Nourish you.
Are taken to heart
that you know I mean
no disrespect
Ultimately you are my inkwell
and a single bloom suffices as quill,
each word more precious than the previous.
All true and earnest and electric.
Patiently you wait until I find my final rhyme
and you ask me to write again
the story of my passion for you
in staccato Morse code
inside.

watch the horizon for signs of life

trade greys for reds and golds and greens.
satin and silk. and all the textures
a kiss can command.
warm, full lips. walking their way
to the mortal portals.
you asked and I was tasked
to bring flowers to a garden.
to kiss the bloom.
petals softly falling.
like angels in rebellion.
show me your wings
my graceful faerie
merry
in the moment
extended into the night
and into the light
for I would more than lay and play,
but walk and talk
and practice the alchemy
that is ours
as it rises with the sun.

Two Feet of Snow in Buffalo

Two feet of snow in Buffalo.
I should be there
to see the flakes settle in your hair,
whatever colour it is this week.
To catch you if you slip on the ice,
or be gracious if you do the same for me.
To make sure you have hot cocoa
when you get home late, half frozen.
To give you a good excuse to call in sick
and spend the night warm and safe,
wrapped in blankets of wool, not frost.
I would like to be there.

Impaired

no. not tonight.
the worse for the wine,
you are impaired
and, to be honest, I am scared
that in the morning
you will not remember.
I will be forgotten
along with the thought processes
that slid you, naked, under the sheets
and brought you to kiss me
with a certain intent.
I will, however, stay the night
and hold you, if you wish.
if in the morning
you still believe
this is a good idea,
I will not leave
until you ask me to
for I want you
and I am unimpaired.
drunk only on your beauty.

Dragons do not rise, the ground falls away

Listen to the sound of blood in your veins.
The pain of life, accumulated scar tissues
and issues with memory and dreams.
The currency of hope. Of pain. Of pleasure
that we measure in teaspoon of numbing,
the dumbing of our voices to the choices
that will be made for us if we do not speak out.
Speak up. Cup our hands and drink deeply
like the mighty men of Gideon. Ready to fight,
whatever the battlefield, whatever the odds,
whatever the gods the pagan parade and serenade
with the screams of the sacrificial lambs.

I bring no balm, no curative salve or oil
to anoint your warm flesh. I am a distraction
from the pain, bringing my own complexities
and vexities, for the moments you grant me.
Fantasies of distant lands and the hands of strangers
that never clench to strike, the peace of release
as the blood drains out to shift red heat
to an acceptable warmth in the interlude
between rude ruttings, an education
in a provisional, positional geometry
of shifting shapes and close escapes
that taste of cinnamon and jasmine.

Comforting ourselves in chaos and bent intent,
recently spent and reinvested against untested
desires and passions fashioned as images
graven and gravure, promises forgotten
and finally kept, swept in and out in taut
and hot prey, caught and drained of pain.
Chased by the dragon, even when unseen,
The keen keenings saved for cloisters
where the oysters are pried apart
and the pearls are kissed in mysteries
our histories predicted in an arc
of lightning striking in obsidian fire.

Patchwork Hearts

Failed and healed. Fates sealed and broken into
by the grave robbers of our own resurrections.
We are the patchwork hearts, the ragdoll golems.
Shambling in soft tread menace down ancient trails
where what we are pales besides what we dare.
Red yarn hair and button eyes, curiosity driving us
to occasionally wander off the path and find fire
really does burn. Pulling on threads we should ignore
as we take risks when we can, take comfort in hope,
and dream dreams as large as patchwork hearts can.

Seduction in G sharp

The words are spun like sugar candy, threads and clusters
of sweet pinkness, mustering the feelings that steal and seal
our destinies, if only for a night, then memories.

You invited me into your life, like the heroine of a novel
where the vampire king is more tragic, more noble
than the young man at the well who brings flowers.

But powers and magic in amomancies fill the air
of the night, like jasmine and honeysuckle
and the curiosity of the furiosity of these passions.

A palette of colours that lay the flush and brush
on the canvas of your heated frame, runes in white
and red bloods, the clarity of true parity and sincerity.

When all is said and done and the sun rises,
all the same there is no shame, no blame,
that we are the agents of our own pleasures.

I will not seduce you, reduce you to a formula
to achieve a goal. You are a flower and a cloud,
beautiful and whole and perfect with or without me.

Legends of songs in a cave

Dragon casting shade!
serenade
me if you will
while I kill time
imagining
what never was
and should have been.
Fingers flying over the frets
of a precision cithara
synchronized to sounds
that barely pass for words
but communicate the quintessence.

Flying Elves

We are ourselves, flying elves
that consider the consequences of our actions.
fractions of multitudes are still a lot,
and we are caught up on the barbs of barbarism,
power feeding our basest shadows.
Flexible flirtations, denigrations
spoken only when the spine is broken
and the limbs entwined barter refined expressions
held in dark corners
to summon our unique alchemistry

Trippingly

More than just words spoke trippingly on the tongue,
stung by lost opportunity, sharper than a slap,
in the lap of a luxurious light, as hot and as bright
as any fire kindled in a spindly-legged beggary.
Sweet, sweet and then some, musky and dusky
is the feast, ceased only by command, demands
drive a lively recourse, intercourse on the tip of the tongue.

Visions without Eyes

We acknowledge the prize is not a single thing,
a kiss or a ring or one more Spring spent to repent
lost opportunities, misplaced rather than erased
from memories that we wish we could deny.
Lola set the bar pretty high and Anais
made a mess of the meandering meanings
when the only truth is found inarticulate
for hours, sheets wet and appetites whetted
as the wholly trinity becomes a challenge
you once gave me, brave of me to remember
when you can't ask for what you want.

Lola Montez

If I was King of Bavaria
would you be my Lola
reminding me of the heat of fire banked
until fed into an inferno, burning vanity and sanity
to ash.
Would you be my courtesan
accept a royal title
vital to my passion, even if many cursed you?
What passes between lovers is not for consensus
or vote.

I will find you

In the labyrinth of your sorrows
the joy of what you are shines.
Nothing and no one is ever truly lost
and resilience is the key to survival.
Give me a clue and I'll look for you.
Give me a sign and I'll find the way.
If only for an instant, only for a touch
only for a moment, to be recalled so much
in my magic and my memory, tapestries spun,
fires burn eternal once they're begun
and you are a sun. A star at a distance
but on closer inspection, not just cold light.

legacy

What do you want from me? A legacy?
A legend? Something to confess in later years
when I am gone and they look for you
to decipher the bread crumbs in my words?
I don't care if you hide behind riddles
as long as you are, with me, true.
Let the psychohistorians lose their minds
trying to find the blind spot in your veil
they can sail around in their illusions
of navigating my sphere, you are here
for now, and even if they never find you,
as long as you come for your own reasons
you are welcome to visit and leave your mark.

shadows and smoke

feed me your fantasies. dark vows in light footfalls,
calls made to serenade my libido. the music of dreams
provoked, invoked and choked out in raspy sighs.
the wheres and whens and whys are irrelevant
as long as the who is you and true to your words.
the scent lingers and I ponder a meal of substance,
not just a menu of promises, of shadows and smoke.
I will touch and take and slake in every oath uttered
to you in transient imaginings when you were hungry
and needed to know the savage ravagery is yours
for the taking, for making your own like fingernail
scars raked to make bloody signatures and sigils
of a spellcraft beyond powders and paints, saints
damned and demanded in a ceaseless release.

in the erotique

Welcome to the erotique, the grown world of grown up words
and shadows that sometimes are prettier than the colours.
Red looks blacker than black and the white shines to the touch
as we drink down our philters and tight sleight of more than hand
grant us ardent gardens of wishes places against the candored lust.
Controlling our darkest angels with red laces and traces of pain,
we cut against the grain to gain control over our souls, deep and hot.
Not for nothing, all for something and the feral faeries command,
demand the sacrifice of the tormented moments bartered for release.

linotte: a contemplation

you flit like whim and brush your wings across my notice,
a poultice for a ravaged heart. trust before dust
and a trace of a dark smile and hunger
shared between two similar avians.
songs of both the leathery and feathery
an urgent urge to surge so deep that sleep
is a memory for lesser creatures.
and heat becomes its own salvation.
little bird with a great thirst.
bursting with white wine gone red
in a bed of thistles and deep desires.

Disease

take me tender on your knees,
share with me our shared disease,
please me with passion and desire.
draw me in to quench your fire.
suckle hard with lips and hips,
take me in throughout the night.
let me hear you scream and swear,
all the way, if you dare.
I will taste and feel your depths,
leave you trembling and deep cleft.
feed on me and I'll oblige.
on your tongue, between your thighs.

Sinister and Sweet

It's a left-handed compliment, an acknowledgement of contemplation
of the corruption your seduction suggests.
Soft skin, full lips, your shoulders, your breasts,
I hope you take requests because
by the end of the evening
I won't be leaving much off the menu.
This can mean something.
This can mean everything. Or nothing.
The decision is yours, I am open to the lashing rain of your pain
and your pleasure, a measure of treasure that can be locked away
or laid bare, like tousled hair on a satin pillowcase, tracing music
with your fingertips in the air.
I am not afraid of your desires,
your fires will not burn me but raise me to an eclectic boil,
spoils and soils
of the toils of this mortal coil
shared and nothing spared if we've shared
the sweet heat and the ravenous ravishings
we both would prefer, truth told.

Public

Taunt me with glimpses of your body, with eye flutter fetishes of flirtation.
You enjoy this, watching me lean hard into the wall to hide my reaction,
the traction of the stone walls barely sustaining my inarticulate delight
that you light the night with bright brisance, silk and satin skins shed
to litter the floor (more or less) as we pour ourselves into the flushing rush
of crush lips and hips and slipping this way and that like cats in a fury.
No hurry, but curious to see when and where this ends, if ever.
Tell me a secret, I'll trade it for a new one, one you'll never admit
even in your scandalous whisperings when I am gone and you still feel
in certain corners of your being, my presence, the pleasance of touch
held just long enough to be insuperable a force and we run our course
loud enough to worry about the neighbors, and laughing about it later.

expressions

that pout.
no doubt it has worked its magic many times on hardier souls that I,
for even before you set your lips to persuasion,
I am your captive, bound to orbit
like a satellite,
locked to always face towards you for signs of awareness
that I am even out here,
cold in the night sky and hidden during the daylight.
you are the rare, fair creature
who is willing to express herself fully,
using the full palette of facial expressions.
you say more than mere words with a look
and your vocabulary is beyond mine,
such that I may need the rest of my life
to compile even a modest fraction
of the nuances of your simplest smile.
or sneer.
or frown.
or pout.
even at rest you are a beautiful puzzle to me.

I linger at the well

I would spend an hour or two or more, merely lapping softly
at the well of life, demonstrating my resolve to seek your joy
and your approval of my attentions.
do not mistake my hunger for lack of desire to pour albino fire
deep inside you in rhythmic gouts of surrender and release,
ceasing only when exhausted.
but, I like it here, the soft taste. the texture. the way you writhe
when I find the right spot and rhythm and say my name
like an epithet of an ancient deity.
the scent of you is jasmine and sunlight, strange counterpoint
to the sunlight of your warm flesh, a feast for the beast within me.
and I would draw great pleasure from yours.

real woman

a woman. a real woman.
an amalgam of a thousand things.
or more.
the scent of honeysuckle and jasmine
between her thighs.
the taste of opportunity on her lips.
the sound of memory in her laugh.
the eclectic lightning in her wit and thoughts.
the touch...
oh, yes, the touch.
her entire body an instrument of music
and profound communication
beyond merely her eyes and smile
and the way her nails and teeth leave marks
when she is at her most sated.
grace personified.
drinker of the white wine
and the echo of the divine nature
of beauty.

In the Heat of the Moment

pink petals on pale skin.
or are they a part of it?
your soft heat radiating
like the aftermath of a dream.
the air is hazy with your scent
and I went a little out of my mind
when you kissed me
with feral intentions
and I felt your thighs against my skin.
silk and satin and linen and lace
falling away or torn aside,
I don't remember which or wish
to dwell on more than this moment.

Feasting on a Lover

I entertain your darkness, as you entertain mine.
Those epic moods are food to my soul, sweet and toothsome.
A fit feast for poets and artists and those brave souls
seeking sustenance in something, someone, more than bland.
More than simple nourishment, boring and lacking spice
to stimulate the tongue and the palette, nutmeg, cloves,
cinnamon and a hint of deeper treasures, heat
that only comes after many courses, when gluttons
slip away to digest what will sustain them, stale bread
crusts that were easiest to obtain. Not savoury
nor deserving to be savoured, flavoured clumsily
with just enough sugar to hide the masala within.
I want the flesh, the blood, the marrow untapped, not wrapped
in an assembly line, a disquieting disguise.

Menu

you have that quality of something that I cannot put to words.
as a poet, this frustrates me, but it also tantalizes me
like smelling something tempting outside an unfamiliar restaurant,
wondering if anything could taste as good as it promises.
knowing to trust my senses and drop my defenses
and get ready for a fresh and new and unique experience.

A Deep and Resonant Purr

I envy cats their ability
to fall asleep in any position
without penalty or agony
the next morning.
But, waking from deep sleep
limbs akimbo
and your naked, merged form
still atop me
where we did not stop lovemaking
as much as fade to a truce
I will gladly barter
a stiff neck
and a leg cramp
for another moment
as part of our whole.

Constant Seductions

we cross the line each in our own manners
throughout a night that fed from evening,
an afternoon filled with intimacies,
a soft morning we found hard intersect.
one of those days (and nights) so rare and fair
that we will hold to each others' account.
whispers. touches. our proof of life complex
with the nature of our very beings.

Midnight Musing

In these quiet and shaded moments I think
of you, even when you are not with me.
Hundreds of miles. Thousands, even, we blink
and the moments pass by, leaves on a tree
that grows too swift for us to do more than
stand back and watch in discomfort that time
will take the path found most convenient and fan
these fires, these new desires, until this rime
is little more than ashes and memory
and we are left to sit in the desert
and ask philosophical questions we
do not want to know the answers to, curt
excuses made for times when I wake you
in the middle of the night and take you.

Immortal

You don't have to lay with me to be immortal.
I barter not such amomancies, for that would
diminish magic of the human heart, portal
to my soul is not beneath sheets of satin, should
the price of passion become a rough coin of brass
it would diminish the value and the virtue
of every kiss and touch, the whispers that pass
for eloquence, quenching fires of ebony hue.
I will not burn forever, but the ash and soot
of my brief flash shall leave a mark in hallowed halls.
The flicker casts shadows in the shape of you, put
to leave your trace on the chaste alabaster walls
I freely mark if now received as communion
or refuse my flesh in sacramental fusion.

Negotiation

I would not need to undress you to impress you.
But I would like to, anyway. To lose myself in you,
as deep as you permit. To not quit when I am sated,
for it is your pleasure I will measure myself against.
Folding memories and daring to lose myself
in merging flesh, purging the demons of doubt.
I am slack-jawed with awe at your beauty, your
essential sensuality and your honest acceptance
of me, not surrender, but a truce of trust.
Negotiations continue through the night
and the treaty may not survive breakfast,
but I am willing to give unilateral concessions
of my touch and thickened penetrations.
Blurring borders as we work towards a lasting peace.

Pale Minstrel

cold fall the petals of the sky upon the earth, the flowers die,
the seasons change their garb and dance along.
I'll capture her with barest trace; her voice, her face, her lethal grace,
in rhyme, in thought, and this small tribute song.

she knows me best who know me least,
makes bread and fishes into feast
and understands the essence of my art.
her form is fair beyond the norm and to her side the suitors swarm
and I have but my distant words, for my part.

haphazard though my tune may be my words are honest
and she can see
my gentle hands pluck out my plaintive tune.
I woo with all that she'll hold and have and offer all and more by halve
in hopes of turning winter into June.

Snowflakes are Imperfect

White.
Delights of crystalline water.
Dancing in the wind.
Hiding the shadows in a sheet of reflected glory.
Such is the story of our hearts.
Damned to melt
when we discover we live in the real world.
Let winter endure
that the rain, impure,
might cover up the sleeping sorrows.
Snowflakes are imperfect
for they are but transient façade.
Seasons go on
for me and for you.
Come Spring
I will come for you.
And demonstrate the beauty of life.

Centigrade

Whatever the scale, the temperature remains the same.
The name does not change the essence, the nature,
of my affections for you. Platonic? Hardly. But patient
as a monk, resigned to the sound of earnest echoes
and the thousand reasons why this would not work.
What you perceive as bitter cold I still read as positive
and the heat lingers, buried perhaps, but it does not lapse
into an unconscious, unconscionable cynicism.
It is merely a matter of where you mark the numbers
when you place the plate behind the glass that passes
for an analog of the dialog we are both sustaining,
entertaining the notions of something far towards
the other end of the scale. Boiling, scalding, searing
possibilities of an arcane heat, against your quicksilver.

Banquet of the Vanquished

I want to get you hungry.
Feral.
The best way to unleash the feast to better consume our fills.
Sating our appetites by whatever means necessary.
Vampyrs in a flood of blood,
red and white,
drawing heat to complete the sweet sweat
with which we initially whet
then wet
our throbbing teeth.
Wreathe us in a turbulent sensation and burn,
burn like bound sacrifices to our own devices.
The price of passion is agony,
raw flesh and the mesh of the deepest measures
of how far we go
and go on,
beyond our perceived limitations,
no more pale imitations
of lust
before the dust has its way
with what we leave
on the table,
barely able to
walk or talk
but the exhaustion is earned.
And the next course served.

My Fine Fae Lady

Invite me now in, into your tender garden,
where rare and unique beauty is to be revealed.
Flowers, leaves, fragrance like honeysuckle, jasmine,
all the sounds of the soft rain of beauty unsealed.
Not requiring, but desiring, a cautious hand,
sturdy plow to help ensure tis not overwhelmed
by vagrant vagaries of intention unplanned.
My fine fae lady, I am not unacquainted
with the rituals of your sprouts, needing the care
of an empathetic gardener, understanding
the necessity of an earnest heart to bear
a sustained effort, your approval demanding
as I press to your beds and lay root where best
to make grow what your heart requires to be impressed.

Not a dream passes

not a dream passes for me
that you are not in residence
maybe you are indeed my future
if not my present tense

making differences on varying scales
knights errant or merely lost
in the chaos of the madness
changing karma for others' cost

trusting Fae will show the way
when the night acquires all our lands
seeking more than just the answers
seeking more than hearts and hands

wishing I could prove my purpose
weirding ways and all and more
praying fate will find me raised up
and not just scattered on the floor

Once again

In the darkness
we see with different eyes
drawing our sight from inner strength.
The texture of your skin is more profound.
Warm. Smooth. Seductive.
Your lips, your hips, feeding me in sips
of what communicates a subtle invitation
amplified and magnified
by the sounds.
Oh my God, the sounds you make
take me to another plateau and drop me:
Slow fall and I crawl to the edge
to beg for another ride.
Inside you is comfort and hunger
softer and smoother and warmer
than the soul of creation.
There is a feral grace in this place.
The scent of your skin.
The taste of your lips.
The texture of your breasts.
The sound of your urgent insurgent utterances.
God's name not in vain
as you drive me insane,
then save me from the madness
once again.

Flash and Fire

flash and fire, the desire is the spark,
dark and dreadnaught. hot as coals
held in your hands just long enough
to burn holes in your soul and you
wake
just long enough to pass out. centimeters
measured against the sky and I
am lost in an uncertain universe
looking for something more than memory.
flash and fire, you inspire me, light
curves back upon itself then burns
cursive holes in the silence of the page.
rage against this cage and take the stage
long enough for one savage dance.
then another. lover who can smother
me with your presence and I drown.
happy.

Driftwood

would you mind if, for tonight, we just lay
beside one another, touching without
expectations of the slow descent, way
to sated exhaustion, ending in rout
of our civilized veneers, animal
seeking creation and recreation.
I love more than your body, held in thrall
by your smile and kind heart, preparation
for the grace of heaven. a prophecy
of peace, of the charity of God's spell,
kindred spirits navigating the sea
of storms, of the mighty waves that will swell
to break us beneath their most brutal tide.
we tread water together, side by side.

The Sonnets of Grace: I

Than any spring of deep earth! Beauty sure!
You are the nature of passion and peace,
argent angel made manifest to cure
the sorrows of my brittle soul, to cease
my greytint memories and bring colour:
Fields of bright blossoms to the horizon!
Fed by the cold mineral water, pure
as a virgin's first kiss, a kind reason
to shield the light of brisant meander
that draws our eyes from the prize of real joy
to find kindred soul to inspire wonder
and break open my heart as an envoy
of fantastic land of dreams envisioned.
I shall surrender worlds unimagined!

The Sonnets of Grace: II

I shall surrender worlds unimagined,
to pale the Duke's gift to his courtesan.
You are more than flesh and fantasy, sinned
and again, altar for my desire, plan
of a seduction to the royal line.
Temptress arcane and alabaster, heat
meets a sweet defeat in your fire divine.
Your flesh is as soft as angel's kiss, sweet
and otherworldly. Penetrative promise
and the persuasion of your innocence,
oil and water heated to precipice
with the true language of romance, defense
I tear aside the lace and silk, false skins,
abdicate my throne and atone my sins

The Sonnets of Grace: III

Abdicate my throne and atone my sins,
ruling in façade, fallen force majeure
to make request to test the truth of skins
in contact to merge, sacred and impure,
lightning in your mouth, your lips are prophets
in the desert of all false lovers' dreams,
the blasphemy of chalk oaths, epithets,
the shadow of panthers and curdled creams.
Ruling from the boudoir, iron scepter
and velvet throne. Lesser immolation
to sheathe heat against the pagan specter
that makes mockery of subjugation.
I would lay aside my red cassock, sinned
to be within your grace, to be the wind.

The Sonnets of Grace: IIII

To be within your grace, to be the wind
that passes through you, leaving trace eddies
that empower and deflower your heart, spinned
dust devils riding out the decades breeze
and cyclone, hurricane and zephyr blown
from the clouds of your beauty to summon
all manner of mischief and legend known
to future generations as some one
who inspired poetry and envy, lust
and worship of pale divinity brought
to life and placed among us to entrust
us with the secrets of the holy, taught
in emancipated flesh, feral skins,
in a desert of barren bones that pins.

The Sonnets of Grace: V

In a desert of barren bones that pins
you to the ground. The sound of the sorrows
of failed lovers, timid tale of the sins
of inadequate passions, tomorrows
cast away for the moment, yet unmoved
by the logic of the heart or the touch
of hands and glands that had not planned unproved
strategies, dependent on blind luck such
that even the gods laugh derisively.
You drew me here to make my sacrifice
on your pale flesh, the spill of white wine, free
of constraints that might taint the boatman's price,
shackled by lips that kiss and hearts that pound
the bravest and the boldest to the ground.

The Sonnets of Grace: VI

The bravest and the boldest to the ground,
bound and tormented, rebellion fomented
in the name of a goddess, an unsound
faith based on predisposed and demented
oaths of belief, grief for lost years and tears
shed red in crevices of memory.
Cinnabar sins, we are yet crippled by fears
that grind us down like harpy's emery,
sharpening the poignant poniard that will
penetrate more than willing hips, the rush,
the crush, the flush of release, little kill
and faint awareness of endorphin push
through to paramour of the romanesque,
we are flesh and blood and the arabesque.

The Sonnets of Grace: VII

We are flesh and blood and the arabesque.
Inconsistency, our consistent trait,
our beauty and grace conquers the grotesque
remnants of our sod-bound uprising, fate
and the sound of dripping wax as time burns.
But your soul is, itself, beautiful.
Time may mark its passage in twists and turns
that lay tracks around your eyes, terrible
demolitions of our bodies and minds,
cursing us our mortality and more.
Even stilled and cold, I would hold the binds
of ancient oaths to your flesh and heart, lore
of my mythos, passion will not unbound
in visions from Poe and Lovecraft, each sound.

The Sonnets of Grace: VIII

In visions from Poe and Lovecraft, each sound,
darkness lingers, stingers in the green fields
where lovers would lay, only to be struck, bound
by dark forces, where hope to madness yields.
I seek a deeper prick than mere nettles,
a transient insanity of blood heated
on and in your altar of where settles
only the red blood and white wine, meted
injustice for the soft to the savage,
a passion play of hungry religion
taking communion in forms that ravage
one another, the merging division
decreed by design, heroes picaresque
echoing in chilled depths of souls, grotesque.

The Sonnets of Grace: VIIII

Echoing in chilled depths of souls, grotesque
though our feral entanglement may seem,
it is not quanta or the picturesque
pretense of an ardent virgin's wet dream,
filled with illusions, misapprehensions
about how it is all supposed to work
when we merge to purge solitude, tensions
uncoiled then soiled in a three-ring cirque
of your surrender and your demands, made
and unmade, the linen, immolative,
consume, itself in shame for what was said
in the ancient tongues of lovers, suasive
in both silence and in eloquence due,
with the malformations we are heir to.

The Sonnets of Grace: X

With the malformations we are heir to
it is miracle that we comprehend
the frailest of our failings, hearts passed through
the baptism of our saddest times, defend
our cynicism with doubt and the cold
calculus of our barnacled souls, hard
as Pharaoh's damnation, denying bold
prophecy and the word of God, long scarred
by our own illusions that we are fit
to pit wits against the fates themselves, mad
with our own pain and gaining no acquit
in insanity pleas, lost hearts that had
fair hope to re-enter the grand circuit:
affection and desire, the live wire.

The Sonnets of Grace: XI

Affection and desire, the live wire,
funeral pyre, the spire of the temple
we throw down from, fulfilling the desire
to both give and take the waking, simple
in the equation, but the prayers are long
and complicated, speaking in the tongues
old before mortals messed it all up, song
of Solomon and Kama Sutra, rungs
of Jacob's ladder, electrocuting
inadequate supplicants on their quest,
their pilgrimage, purging the polluting
perfume of forgotten blossoms to test
purest of scalds; skalds speak our legend, true,
that grounds us to the beauty we are due.

The Sonnets of Grace: XII

That grounds us to the beauty we are due,
and this finds our paths a laughing torment.
between the poles and pages we wage new
dogmas: Who we are and deserve, torment
of our inner selves and shelves of scribblings
of mad philosophies of God and love
that burn away and give to the nibblings
of the vermin that infest us, above
the marquee moments we aspire to,
demanding our due and paying our dues
in currency of colding kisses, true
to our pretensions, our hearts we will bruise
before bursting into eloquent fire,
letting slip flip platitudes of desire.

The Sonnets of Grace: XIII

Letting slip flip platitudes of desire.
More on my lips than words, your sweet essence
drips in sated statement of rutting gyre
as you cry out to prove that my presence
meets your criteria for further feasts.
I make no command, no barter demand
of treasure for treasure, for heated beasts
do their natures and I will gladly stand
glad to enter whatever covenant
you offer me, patience is the virtue
of the lover. Reticence resident
shall vacate to make room for me, anew.
Here is proof of my inspiration, sure.
There is truth in my eloquence, more pure.

The Sonnets of Grace: XIIII

There is truth in my eloquence, more pure
than any tantalus flood, a spring struck
by a prophet to demonstrate the cure
of despair is hope and prayer, beyond luck
in the toss of the dice, the price of fools.
Luck is but persistence in random
models of chaos theory, dreary rules
describing a universe near awesome
as the peace of your presence, evidence
of something grander than science, the glim
of the less dim options over the fence
into infinite plains of daisies, rim
of oceans we swim to, more sweet and pure
than any spring of deep earth! Beauty sure!

The Sonnets of Grace: Diadem

I shall surrender worlds unimagined.
Abdicate my throne and atone my sins
to be within your grace, to be the wind
in a desert of barren bones that pins
the bravest and the boldest to the ground.
We are flesh and blood and the arabesque
in visions from Poe and Lovecraft, each sound
echoing in chilled depths of souls, grotesque
with the malformations we are heir to.
Affection and desire, the live wire
that grounds us to the beauty we are due,
letting slip flip platitudes of desire.
There is truth in my eloquence, more pure
than any spring of deep earth! Beauty sure!

from the book **Cleave** (coming together):

photo of and by Mariya Andriichuck, 2015

cleave William F. DeVault
poetry 1972-2011

Strange...but Beautiful

strange but beautiful
the arc of the lark, a curve of unswerving passion
fashioned in jasmine and honeysuckle wreaths
to stop the nosferatu's teeth
from more than a taste
from laying waste
to what, in haste, was imagined love
and some immortal dream of joy
that mirrored what I'd seen in the sun's cleft,
or so I imagined, in hope God had left,
but it came from blood
not the ether that folds cold memory
into the shrouds of distant stars
the better to bind noble scars
strange but beautiful

strange but beautiful
I can sense your presence
but I cannot ken the vector of your approach
and like Hector, I cannot fight
what I cannot touch in the light
swinging blind against the walls
as I kick against the pricks
I would place palms to cool stone walls
and wait your arrival, eyes shut to silence
the shadows of the fires
the shadows of desires
that would blacken flesh and bone
and drag me to the precipice
to dance for the fates my amomancies
strange but beautiful

Base Sacraments

I am not God.
for God does not need
to taste
the sweat of your kisses
to remind him of
your nature
your dreams
your needs
your beauty.
God is above the stirring
in my loins
whenever you smile
and a small strand of hair
falls askew to remind me
of how you look
stretched out beneath me
at the center of
a heated joy.

And.

I would prefer to worship you
than be worshipped by you,
as I draw purpose from your pleasure.

I Stand for You

I stand for you and lay for you as wills your perfect heart,
plucked from the Earth by time and toil to fulfill patient cause.
I beg from you an answer true to my bold suit and part.
For diamond hearts and passioned priests the truth is as a dart
that pierces deep while mortals sleep to lay the pathway's laws.
I stand for you and lay for you as wills your perfect heart,
I knew your soul had struck a toll when witnessed from the start:
A dutied beauty in the stone ripped out by careless claws.
I beg from you an answer true to my bold suit and part.
I bleed out love to wash away the stains life would impart
and purify the petty lies the fools would curse as flaws.
I stand for you and lay for you as wills your perfect heart,
The waves will roar and tides may ebb but I shall stand apart
from sounding seas and soul's disease that would give others pause:
I beg from you an answer true to my bold suit and part.
I am not here for a fraction less than what fulfills my art,
and your kiss matters more to me than any crowd's applause.
I stand for you and lay for you as wills your perfect heart,
I beg from you an answer true to my bold suit and part.

Thin Skin

warm your heart on the heat of my hands
as I span long moments spreading oils
and lotions of fragrance on your thin skin.

my eyes closed, in wonder, at your softness.
your eyes closed, in wonder, at my warmth
and the peculiar sensations my touch invokes
to be explored later, with more than hands
and nothing between us
but hope.

The Satyr's Suit

stay with me a while.
lay with me a while.
play with me a while
and I will make you smile

to the best of my ability.

I will worship you tonight,
in the darkness, in the light,
whate'er to you seems right.
or, at least, to your desire...

let me touch and taste your fire.

let my hold you and explore.
let me give you all, and more,
let me shake you to your core,
let me take you, make you, break you

of all sorrows and lost fantasies.

I will earn your memory.
I will turn you, set you free.
I will burn your depths, as we
explore all the pleasures, once denied

you have had to hold inside, waiting for me.

Genii

I don't want to disappoint you
but with my sweat to anoint you
as I labour for your pleasure
and I savour your delight.

let me peel your self-denial
and just lay back for awhile
let me measure you for memory
while I treasure your release.

for the joy that I will generate
will seem radiant as I penetrate
into corners of your spirit
where now mourners congregate

I am called by invocation
to achieve a consummation
to slide deep into your body
til you sleep as ne'er before

with your fragrant garden tended
and your broken heart well mended
you can rest within my arms
until your cresting hunger calls

Aside, Astride the Phoenix

bid me enter to your sphere
but tell not the world as I draw near
that I have come to meet you here -
aside, astride the phoenix.

speak to me not the shallow myths
of words that fell from ancient cliffs
to fill the valleys, full of glyphs
of warning, warding, wonder.

behold my breath, it burns the wind,
that whips through fields where lovers twinned
and bade brave bliss for sinners skinned
to feel each healing heartbeat.

that you have dared is proof enough
that you are made of earnest stuff -
cuir bouilli, smooth and tough,
to shield the unhealed warrior.

enter freely, of your will,
that you may share in what we spill
then gather up, to drink our fill
of the flooded blood of passions.

Behind the Façade

behind the facade
where
you kissed me
once
violating
promises
you and I had made
to ourselves
and each other
not to mention
other people
who seemed
suddenly irrelevant
at least for the moment
when lips touched
and something
-something-
arc'd
like lightning
but much
much
more pleasant
which suddenly seemed
a very faded word
and everyone
who wasn't there
that is to say
who wasn't me or you
only saw a red glow
on the horizon
and weren't sure
if they heard thunder
because you kissed me
behind the facade.

The Priest of Passion Serves the Sacrament

break me down
take me down that shadowed path
where we once lingered,
daring fate to let us
touch
in ways shown sharing
in ways known caring
about what wordless whims
were communicated.

I can smell
your attar on my hands and clothes,
ancient faded memories
that I summon freely
heat
that feeds this fire
that feeds this desire
and when you shed your veils
I will enter the temple.

deity
and the temptress to my fall,
all I have - I sacrificed
the price of your hunger
fed
to make me bleed
to take my need
and let me mark a holy scripture
in fingertips on your flesh.

The Goddess Walks

the goddess walks in her garden
unaware that the sun is waiting her whim,
grim moments lending impetus to joy,
a royal smile on lips known to taste tears.
some where in the distance, where dark
gives way to grey and time holds sway
only for those foolish enough to mark it,
a troubadour plays a sweet and barren ode.

she shall serve as sacrifice
when forgotten gods of love and lust
call for their avatar,
surrendering her heart
to rule a land measured only
in how far I will walk in dreamless sleep
between now and the end of all things,
making words into wonders for as long
as there is language for a song.

for sacrifice empowers dreamers and lovers,
that which hovers between birth and death
a baby's breath in colours resplendent,
transcendent o'er all things, even pain,
as the power of light and shadows
weaves threnodies into amomancies
and nothing is regent but her will.

for I have waited this long for this song,
this song of stone and clay and fire and water,
this song of memory and hope.
praying for transfiguration as an act of will,
left behind as the kill of a nosferatu's rage.
laying page to wound to stem the life
that shall not serve as Ouranos' legacy.

Centaur

let me walk to the horizon
with you there by my side.
I'm not looking to play martyr
to some self-consuming pride.

I would ask you many questions
and answer all you dare.
I will smile at life's imperfections
as you brush aside your hair.

there are places on this highway
better spanned by teams of two,
and I am just to thinking
what it would be like, with you.

let me walk to the horizon
with you there by my side.
I've got gas enough for miles to go
if you come along for the ride.

I've got baggage by the bushel
as I know you've got as well,
I can't promise you good weather
but I'd walk with you through Hell.

dreams of the damned and dramas
are better lived in lover's arms
where you're shielded from the fire
by my passion and cast charms.

let me walk to the horizon
with you there by my side.
let us sleep in fields grown feral
where no hunger is denied.

let me walk to the horizon
with you there. by my side.

Aubergine Confession

I would trade my white for your red.
My distance for your bed.
A kiss where e'er you've bled.
And I am yours, forever.

You hold me in your sphere.
I cannot flee from here,
from all that I hold dear:
And I am yours, forever.

Move closer in the cold
and fear not growing old,
our dreams, for time, are sold.
And I am yours, forever.

There is room for pain
that cuts against the grain,
but love, it shall remain,
and I am yours, forever.

I cannot promise fate
will open every gate,
and if I must, I'll wait.
For I am yours, forever.

Dance Naked in the Sky (For the Right Set of Lips)

split second timing
turn on a dime and
find the prime number at the top
burn the walls to the ceiling
leave the world reeling
don't dare start unless you can't stop

climb the wire
light the fire
and dance naked in the sky
live like a goddess
no time to get modest
it's a crime if you just try to get by

show me a reason
to know that your teasin'
is an invitation to dance in the sky
I don't like to take chances
on third string romances
just tell me when and I'll never ask why

climb the wire
light the fire
and dance naked in the sky
come, don't you falter
take me to your altar
for the right set of lips I would die

Faerie: Love

seeing you
just seeing you
fills me with such a sense of
something
I can only recall
if I stretch back my memories
to a time when

love

was not a proven path
to the fate's wrath
and I believed
still believed
in the happy ending
at the end of a story of

love

what is the manner of
this mystery
this magic
this amomancy
that have you shrouded me with
so that I would dare to care to

love

when around every corner
on every shelf
in every empty pocket
I have evidence enough
of the bristlethorn nature
of the pleasant madness
of daring to

love

In the Strangest Corners of Memory

I will find you in the strangest corners of memory.
The way you took your drink and the pattern
of cool drops of sweat that formed on the glass
as we spoke of nothing as foreplay to
an inevitable union, moments in the future.

The texture of the skin on your back when...
when you were warm and full of life and me.
The way your hair fell in my face when I was
too busy with other things to notice, but remembered
later, and smiled a slow and gentle memory.

The scent of jasmine filtered through the oils
of your skin as you lay beside and beneath me
asking for nothing more than everything I had
and was and would ever be and I gave it all
in joy and hope and dreams and passion undismayed.

The texture of your kisses and the questions you asked
with hands and arms and lips and legs and sounds
that were not words but spoke infinite eloquences
that stole my heart and soul and memory of promises
I had made before I saw your eyes and lost the pain of life.

Kiss Me

kiss me
fear me not for I want something else
than your life.
I want your soul, your heart,
your warm skin and heated blood
to sustain me and fill me.
to warm my lips
and fill my lungs with your surrender.
to bring me to the surface
that I may know the taste of life
if only for the moments
that it remains with you.
remembering that you,
knowing it would mean your death
yet in the knowledge of my desire
that runs to love and passion
you could not press lips
to seal your fate and my hunger
and had the courage and desire to
kiss me

I Find

maybe I will see you sometime
when the skies are bright enough to resolve
the colour of your hair, inviting touch and much,
much more into this sore heart, ancient it seems
at times and then you step into my dreams
and make a mess of my resolution. the evolution
of man to stone is thrown out and I find
I find
an oddly familiar heat within me, when it should not be,
for it died a season or ten ago, a slow death,
fried in the workaday electricity of grounded thoughts.
but you intrigue me in ways I didn't realize
I could still wonder on when I see the image of you,
a smile against blue skies where lies
are sooner or later overturned and burned fingers
heal to conceal all but the memory of pain.
you wake me from the fading light and I find
I find
that the night is not a time for shadows
but the touch of you. a consummation to be wished
like I wish for air and the sun to rise in the morning,
warning me that there are still days ahead
when what I have bled with be remembered to me.
for such is the legacy of the brave.
you make me willing to face the memories
and make new ones, true ones, a few ones
that we really can't explain, you had to be there
but if you were we wouldn't have been doing that
the way we're doing that. when I think of you I find
I find
I want to see just how good all my other senses
can feel when my defenses are down and it isn't
a game or the same old patterns of habituated kisses
when cupid misses and hits other organs besides the heart.
I would lose myself within you to have found
have found
the truth about the religion of love and lovers.

Thunder of Lust

I want to be the consecration of all your hesitation.

I'm not looking to seduce you
or in words to reproduce you
as a shadow of a light that burns so bright.
I'm not heading for a showdown
with my urges, dark and lowdown.
and won't walk away if you want to talk away the night.

There is thunder to lay under
as the light of heaven leavens
all our baggage, for a moment, lost and tossed.
I'm not looking just to use you
or in words to ruse, confuse you,
but know you glow, immolation worth the cost.

I want to be the consecration of all your hesitation.
I want to be the first, the last, the best and more.
I want to be sent reeling off the walls and off the ceiling
and to find my mind defined within your core.

I'm not spitting out excuses for the shadowdancer muses
that seemed bright while I lingered in the night,
barely living but for the sorceries of the dream.
I'm just ready for the static to be more than cinematic,
to reach this nosferatu heart with surging, purging light
that burns away the mocking memories with photic scream.

Yielding to Temptation

yielding to your fantasies.
skies don't lie and I,
I am caught in your cotton candy kisses,
held soft and aloft
like a prayer that dares eyes to caress
each curve with nervous nakedness
of heart and satin skin,
thin to the osmosis of dreams.
yielding to temptation,
crossing boundaries that bind
and blind me to my promises to be good.
bare feet on infinite sheets of sand
that are more than just a place
to trace our illusions,
the winds whipping us to crown senses drowned
in the elegant whispers
that remind us of what we really yield to.

My Passion, My Cathedral

I would lay you down in a bed of soft satin, silks and rare pelts,
a worthy place to trace our passions for a night's mystery,
the history we make more vital than the promises we break,
words lost in a sound of breath and small death to transfigure.
We slip from the shadows to touch and taste and waste not wanting
that had been haunting us from the first inconvenient question
that we did not speak but shared in a furtive glance that dealt
all our cards to a table you alone could see, in front of me,
no barriers to harrier your complicated soul. A thirst to slake
in uncursed waters, blessed and pressed to and into you, pure
and sure as any christened sacrament in a cathedral, prayers taunting
us as words that swelled to let us meld into a shared possession.
For I take naught what I do not give in turn and full, to share,
to bear and bare all you would take into you, as much as you dare.

You are a Charity to This Sphere

The thorns you've worn and earned and well,
from liars, cheats and dogs of Hell
that lay (or sought) beside, inside, and fled
from promises made in a jading bed.
But all are not as bent as those
who made their choice and folly chose
to be their path, and earn your wrath
and prize their lies with evil laugh.
There are those who dare to hold
more than flesh, more than moments sold
for less than told, to cast adrift
this precious soul, this precious gift.
For you are a charity to this sphere,
of this I am certain, that you are most dear.

The Pluck of Pan

I wonder, sometimes, why I feel such draw
to be closer to you. Closer with every throb
of my heart, pounding in my ears, staging a thaw
in those cold corners I swore never to rob
of their well-earned silence, experience
having been a hard teacher and love is sweet
and bitter and complicated, a gentle dance
with violent intentions as I know I will meet
great pain on the road. Not that I do not
think you not worth a hard knock or a hundred,
for I can smell your skin from here, sweet and hot
and waiting for my touch and kiss, remembered
in memories of a future that I may not find
in this lifetime. Your gentle heart, perfect
to the shape of the wounds that life confined
to me in its own mock, dreamt of in lust and respect.
Not the respect of a saint, for I have dreamt
of carrying you away and laying with you, with fire
and a savage affection that would preempt
any notion of a platonic thought, a feral desire
only made sense of inside you, feeling you surrender
to the pleasures of my hardened resolve, seeing you
as your eyes close in your own consummations, tender
and mad, your voice murmuring prayers made true
by your very presence in my heart, my arms, my bed
where I would curse the memory of every other woman
who has pretended to the heart on which you have fed
and found in me something worth the pluck of Pan,
giving over to the need to feed on a lover's breath,
his small death to bring you back to life as yours
awakens in him that which slept, having leapt
in foolish impatience, but now your touch cures.

Abdication

Forgive me my soft sins, a man may fail.
But in malice, I am innocent, grave
may be my demeanor, but passions pale
when measured against my purposed and brave
affections for you. Respect and passion,
immeasurable and of a treasure
unearthed only by your beauty, I've won
nothing in this life if not the pleasure
of your sweet presence in my day and night
until the end of all things. You are birth
and death, the breath of angels in their flight
as they consider a man's word and worth.
I have given mine, and am content I
will lay with you alone, until I die.

The Forge of Aphrodite

like well-earned sweat:
wet.
we set to settle for nothing short of radiance
in the heat of our mutually assured seduction.
penetrate my consciousness and impale me
on your soul, as deep as you can get.
feral,
wrap your legs and lock me in, in a skin we twin
and thin membranes cannot hold back what we are:
a sanctity of desire
fire burning away the grey
until all that is left is white hot flesh and pink,
solferino cravings, engravings on memory in sound and fury,
the jury of our own needs, bleeding the
taste
of jasmine.
I want to feel you,
heal you,
peel you and
conceal you
from all the pain but this:
that we are ephemeral
and all that passes in this heated moment will pass,
glass smooth water to hide the crest of crashing waves
that radiate from within you to
capture
my flesh and fluid.
druidic rituals of fertility and transition,
pagan
perfection
as you take possession of my
soul
and my erection,
laying your claim in a passionate frame and flame
that
licks
away the impurities
in the forge of Aphrodite.

Paramour and Nothing More

An essence spun of red honey and of nightshade.
Paramour, and nothing more, golden fleece and jade.
Dreams drawn like fevered blood by leeches from a soul.
A kiss denied and deified to play its role,
lovers lost, crossed to toss their lust to dust and coal.
An essence spun of red honey and of nightshade.
A touch, a glance, a spirit's dance, so unafraid
to leap from the shadows to merge and purge the shade,
dreams drawn like fevered blood by leeches from a soul.
Thoughts given tongue, tongue given flesh and all control
surrendered like an illusion of virtue, stole.
An essence spun of red honey and of nightshade.
Every player acts, every actor played

a hand or made us what we are, our penance paid,
dreams drawn like fevered blood by leeches from a soul.
I want nothing more than the paramour not fade
on waking, not of just illusion but the whole.
An essence spun of red honey and of nightshade.
Dreams drawn like fevered blood by leeches from a soul.

I Will Pass through the Fire

I will pass through the fire
my flesh clinging to my bones
the smell of ozone and burnt hair
my lash-less eyes reopened
to see with an even greater clarity and charity
I will pass through the fire
for your love

I will pass through the fire
my hands torched and scorched
my feet bare and blistered
my silent tongue loosened
to speak of the moment when I broke with life
I will pass through the fire
for your love

I will pass through the fire
my coeur rage waging war with self-preservation
the hesitation I once felt, melting
my doubts, I have lived a good life
and if this is the final gate, I have no regrets
I will pass through the fire
for your love.

Hephaestus to Aphrodite

You are beautiful.
I, deformed.
A god, no doubt, but not one
that they burn fragrant oils
to gather the favour of.
I am unworthy of you,
unworthy of your love.
It burns within me, this passion,
and yet it burns before me
that for all bonds and bindings
you will never really love me.
Just the idea of me.
The lame god, in the forge of souls,
hammering shape to metals
I have drawn out of lifeless stone.

You are beautiful.
I, deformed.
Cyrano suffered thus, and ultimately
it cost him the woman he loved,
who would have loved him back,
I suspect (ask Apollo, he would know).
But he was man and she, woman,
we burn at a higher degree,
our passions set fire to the skies
and people run and scream and dream
that their hearts could survive such heat.
But they are not that sturdy.
You seek balance in my malformations.
You laugh and smile and feign passions
beyond the novelty of my hideous countenance.

You are beautiful.
I, deformed.
For all your beautiful words and soft touches,
I know what and who I am. I know the smell
of burning sulphur under my nails and know
that my kisses are that of a brute, a thing.
Not a god, which is what you deserve.
I am twisted and I know my place.
Those things which I craft, that is what is sought
by those who follow the twisting labyrinth
into the hot bowels of the Earth to find me.
Lovely ornaments of silver and alloys I alone
can make and master, for I am Hephaestus.
But that does not make me beautiful.
That does not make me worthy of a goddess.

Angels Sleep

angels sleep a shift when we repose,
knowing that life goes on and that even sentinels
must nod from time to time.
and, knowing that I am safe in your arms,
and you in mine,
they need not watch every moment.

I saw you dance, unconsciously, listening
to Ani DiFranco sing about leaving in the morning
and the futility of shyness
when the clock runs short, like a dead end road
between the towers of downtown Los Angeles.

so, ride with me if you dare
ride with me if you care
ride with me, and your hair
will shine with the jewels you tossed
in small hand across the open fields
when you stopped to contemplate three wishes
already well on their way to being granted,
by being planted in my garden.

Brisant Revelations

expect the apocalypse
if a vow as sacred as I have taken
should prove
mutable in the wills
and winds
and currents of the human heart,
stolen from the fires of a Promethean glory
unshackled to the punishing stone
to atone for the arrogance of hope
and love
and empowering the juggernaut.
actions refracted in colours of a spectrum
that runs not from red to violet
but from osmium to radium
through silver and platinum and gold and rhodium
polished to a rosary of alpha particles
striking ghostly glowing receptors
in a flint and steel approach to making
nuclear fusion of lovers' sweat.
breaking down the waters
to make hydrogen and oxygen,
breathing in the latter
and fusing the former
in a thermonuclear glory
that rises like the sun in a heart
finally released like Glatisant
to stalk the legends of a lost mythology.
where the Gods walk only in tandem.
as it should be.

Close Your Eyes

close your eyes
that you do not see the walls dissolve
beneath the silent tears I shed
as I reach out and brush trembling lips
with trembling lips
that seek to speak a truth I have not words
well made enough to communicate.
but can speak with touch so eloquently.
if you will but close your eyes.

Tip for Tap

tip for tap. the crush and thrust of contact made,
displayed, paraded in a prayed-for instinct of distinction.

run red, the heart is bled.
run red, the heart is bled.
and all that I have said
is to get you into bed.

chaste chasings on the framework of folly, ornate
to innate feelings. irate thought censors sent packing.

run red, the heart is bled.
run red, the heart is bled.
and all my passions, dead,
awake to mourners, fled.

crimson lips to solferino folds, gold to the barter,
the starter's pistol for my heart discharges rainbows.

run red, the heart is bled.
run red. the heart is bled.
and these thoughts are all wed
by a weaving of romantique's thread.

tip for tap, the crush and thrust of contact made,
displayed, paraded in a prayed for instinct of distinction.

Dare We Cross the Rubicon?

dare we cross the Rubicon
that lays behind your door?
where sheets and skin and perfumed sin
shall draw us from the floor?
topple our frail dignities
of manners and restraint.
proves to us this fiery rush
is no false suitor's feint?

would you dare to see my scars
that run beneath the veil?
would you dare release your dreams
and climb, where others fail
to hold their breath until their death
is crescent to their prayers?
both barefoot and bare headed, bold,
to climb celestial stairs.

where heaven waits behind the gates
and passion is the key.
where wanting all is not the fall
if you trust your destiny.
dare we cross the Rubicon
that lays behind your door?
where sheets and skin and perfumed sin
shall call us, evermore.

How Would You have Me Touch You?

how would you have me touch you?
how soon? how oft? how soft?
would you have me lay back on the bed
and let you rise, aloft?

would you ask I play seduction
so that you can play ingenue?
or would you like to take the lead
and teach me a thing or two?

shall I wine and dine and sweep you
off your feet and on your back?
or shall this be a blue jeans thing
or a tryst of a darker tack?

may it be to your great pleasure
if I insist your essence kissed,
that I may wait to penetrate
until you have found your bliss?

and would you let me hold you
for the night, or for a while,
and feel the heat between us
and taste the comfort of my smile?

how would you have me touch you?
how soon? how oft? how soft?
would you have me lay back on the bed
and let you rise, aloft?

Jasmine and Plumeria

I will
pass my heat
through oils and essences
held in my hand
just long enough to
pass my heat
into your skin.
your soft
fragrant
skin.
every pore
every curve
every nerve
begging touch
like a child
seeking reassurance.
and as I
pass my heat
into you, the alchemy
begins and the thin skin
turns oil
into gold
that you hold,
every fold,
every plain and ridge
and tensing membrane
calling my name
in silent
invocation
celebration
consecration.
as I dare
pass my heat
into your fires.

The Philosophy of Dreams

touch me. for I am flesh, as you,
given to the same needs for air and food
and warmth, communicated between two bodies
at rest, touching in all aspects possible.
and many improbable,
as I pull a cat out of the quantum corner
and make it into roses to bloom in arcs
of every colour of a spectrum of another sphere
as they fill the room with exotic perfumes
I brought back with me on a trip to the stars.

sing for me. I will smile and touch your hair
and dare to sing along, when I know the words.
for we are at best in blended voice and thought
and flesh, yes, I recall mere moments ago
when I could not tell the terminus between
your light and my darkness, as angels averted eyes
and we made the case for unity between us.
it was. yes, it was. it was something I will write of
when I catch my breath and I can find words unique
and perfect and passionate enough.

dream of me. for I dream of you. I dreamt of you
even before I heard your voice. before I knew your name.
when all I knew was that, by the same evidence that I know
that there is a God, you exist and existed and I would find you,
even if I had to climb mountains of madness and sail,
sail forever, it seemed, on seas of the mediocrity of life.
for there is too much to be lost to the world if I was right.
if love is and was and will be regent. regret wets sweated sins.
but I am a penitent pilgrim, lost on the road to Golgotha.
seeking something more than the philosophy of dreams.

Damascus, Movement 7

"Humble seulement en face de Dieu."
And so the great I Am must have loaned
a reasonable likeness to you.

For I am humbled. Cut down to size,
a bite size morsel for digestion
in the gullet of the phoenix.

The image of the Maker reborn
in graceful secrets, a sadness set
in stones of jet and jade and sapphire.

I have cut the stones we selected.
I have kissed the hems of the elected.
I have sheathed the souls, unprotected.

Wings drawn to launch pirouettes to land
amid dry stones and forgotten bones
left on the desert floor by the road.

Afterimages of shadowdance.
Bright shades casting calculated crimes
in stark relief of the honored dead.

"Humble seulement en face de Dieu."
So the prophecy and loss, counted
in killing stones, is crushed to the crust.

Sacraments in a cul de sac sent
skimming over the bleached beach sand dunes
that stretch far and away into hope.

I cast the runes in riddles, rhythm'd
to force slow staccato memory
to telegraph the tempest tonight.

I will worship with my memories,
I will worship with my threnodies,
I will worship with my vanities.
Zeus and Apollo, Odin and Thor,
small gods of passion, small gods of war,
acolytes on acid etch the night.

Futility folds a hand of prayer
and draws, to an inside straight, a queen
to take the place of fours and knaves.

"Humble seulement en face de Dieu."
I will touch the face of God tonight,
and offer earnest prayers in the dark.

William F. DeVault   QUINTESSENCE

Wine

touching softly the fringe of your hairline, testing the holy waters
of the sweat that forms on your brow, even when it is cool,
as the fool rushes not in this time, but begs the wine
of an earnest heart to age to full flavour and ripe with intoxication
made manifest in the last kiss I place on lips begging
to be crushed so that the juices may flow from the cask
and down the winestems set slightly apart
until the toast is given and the thirst is driven
from us in a wave of warmth made effervescent
by sacred words spoken between the press of life.

Dram

the smallest unit.
beauty and terror
in trace amounts....
it counts for little to our senses.
but its impact is immeasurable,
for it is undetectable and thus
gets past our guards.
shards of the fractured crystal heart
of a forgotten dragon.
flechettes that forget nothing
for they are soulless,
like so many lovers.
but I have seen your fire.
even banked, it burns on...
and I will warm myself one day
when amotions are again allowed
in the dreams of the waking dead.
until then,
let us drink our drinks of trace elements.
and I will teach you alchemy of the heart.

Damascus, Movement 3

aphrodite
does not barter her beauty
for hollow promise.
wisdom girds glib eloquences in a veil of truth,
the sooth that soothes us
like the blood of aloe fresh cut from a garden
where we swore we would never walk again.
jasmine.
a thought slides like electric lovers
across a sea of tranquility
where the dust is kicked skyward
by the blue flames and boots of the explorers.
I awaken from the dream.
sightless.
paralyzed.
the cold catalepsy illustrating the fear of death
I had forgotten.
but there is an incandescence in the darkness.
and, for once, I sink back to sleep,
aware of God.
and cognizant of the pattern in the tapestry
as I await Rome.
content that Damascus was no illusion
this time.

Sparks, Like Frozen Lemons

caught at first glance.
a chance attraction
like a wanderer between stars
caught in the gravity well
of your incandescent eyes.

a sweet smell that draws me in,
seven powers invoked to choke
my last struggles.
a vanity to guard a sanity long lost.
the cost of a vagabond heart.

sparks struck. the kindling catches.
and it matches the fire sweeping
across the dry grass of a solitary soul.
fed by the wind of dreams returning
like the dragons on the horizon.

In the Arms of the Dragon

I kiss the beauty of your complexities.
your scars are a familiar terrain
to my lips, cut as they have been
a thousand times for greater
and lesser crimes unpenanced.
I do not doubt your beauty
and in the arms of the dragon
you fit like a gem in the forehead
of a smiling Buddha, alive and dreaming
of new winds yet to blow and yet
you seem to know where, if not when
they will take you, make you
all that you are already in the arms of the Dragon.

A Summoned Fire

claim for me your tattered soul
that leads your form to wander, soft,
on bare feet to the window's light
(to shroud your curves in barest light)
that I should send dark prayers aloft
to be with you, and play a role,
of conquered and the conqueror:
the paramour you can't forget,
who brought his heart without remorse
to walk your life like challenged course,
and share with you, without regret,
a passion damned forevermore.
allow me all that I desire
and I will share a summoned fire.

Monument

I crave a cup. a bowl. a mug of your heart's steel.
unsheathed before by mortal or god for rage or lust
of things both unneeded and forever unreal...
it is the quintessence...and the dust.

dreams do not stand before you and call the blade.
dreams do not walk or breathe or love you as I do.
and can. and will, if given just a moment's shade
from the moon of pain and the stars that lie.

my words shall be eternal. syntax monuments of you.
beneath the tread of centuries, stone shall fall.
paint peel. music rise to ears long deaf. but now...
and from this night on...you are immortal.

The Unicorns

Please come awhile, remain and play.
The unicorns won't come today.
The faeries and their virtued kin
shall stay away, to paint my sin.
with ancient red and angry fire.

Please come to me and linger, please.
I do not mock, I dare not tease.
Just bring with you an honest smile
and share with me, for all the while,
a love of life and true desire.

The unicorns no longer guard
the meadow just beyond my yard.
They snort with shame and true disdain
upon a hope of ages' pain
and brand me, by their pride, a liar.

The Faceted Sphere: One

the comfort of your kiss. so innocent
that unicorns could watch without grief.
so tempting that, for a moment, a brief
aroma of brimstone flirted with my senses.
there is mystery here, mystery and madness
that begs me to hide from the call of questions
best left unanswered and unasked...veiled confessions
that carry within themselves passion and sadness.
an ending without a beginning...an embrace shared
by lovers in an alternate reality passes by.
and beyond.
the riddle smiles at us and we smile coyly at bonds
that cannot hold us in this sphere...
dreams and nightmares undared.

from the book **Cleave** (splitting apart)

Nemicorn

...and in my willful innocence I slit the fragile throat
of the Dreamhart, the nemicorn that bore me to my Rubicon.
Its blood, a shaft of crystal whispers, gave amotation
to the feelings I feared, and slew, out of time now gone.

the sniggering empaths capered no more, but lay in pain
among the orchids...crippled by the nemicorn's gentle
acceptance of my treachery and butchery. that placid brain
caring not for a vengeance of the visceral.

Dreamhart knew that time would slay me, time and regret
that would be mine when my all-too mortal form failed
in the icy waters, when I found my strength was set
against powers beyond me. when passion paled.

...and in my willful innocence I slit the fragile throat
of the Dreamhart, the nemicorn that bore me to my Rubicon.
Its blood, a shaft of crystal whispers, gave amotation
to the feelings I feared, and slew, out of time now gone.

My Electric Lady

dance for me, my electric lady.
sing a song that gently soothes my soul.
tomorrow I must leave your world again, my love…
as I strive to reach this endless journey's goal.

I once gave up my poor and mortal birthright,
so that I might touch the sky and see true things.
my love, I'm not so sure I would have started,
if I could have seen the pain this voyage brings.

once again, my electric lady,
touch me and bring forth my too-rare smile.
for the moment I am just another mortal-
and a little love will last me quite a while.

if we had only met before the present,
and what is gone had made me what I am,
a love would be that all who live might envy-
but I cannot come back this way again.

for the final time, my electric lady…
give me all that I may take within my vow.
tomorrow is my child and a gift to the stars-
and the night is just my brother here and now.

The Reich of Self-discipline

you are alone because you choose to be alone.
I am alone because you choose to be alone.
the balance is not there, but the justice is.
truth like a peach,
crimson with overripeness,
nectar oozing in rivulets of pink sweetness
not unlike the last feast of passion I will ever taste.
memories unerased by the passage of time,
the message of crime uncommitted.
unremitting love.
sad.
as sad as a clock's song of solace.
less than the truth, more than a lie.
we cry in corners hidden from the watchful eyes
of our internal, eternal, infernal critic.
epic and poetic epigrams that slam doors
of opportunity as the fruit
slowly
slides
from its anchorage and
falls.
falls.
falls from the summit of dark kisses
and the joy of love play
into the isolation of the hard earth
amid the bitter blades of sawgrass
and the Reich of self-discipline.

The Common Tongue

the orthography of poets
belongs in poetry.
not in words spoken
in pain or anger or fear
of losing something or someone
held so dear
that you feel death upon you.
that is a time for the babysteps
of simple words, where commonality
is more likely true. a basic
tongue where truths are not
garbled amid the noise of well-meaning
friends who read letters like
Rorschach tests and listened that night
you raved until late, finding hate
in wounded love and bitter tears.

Will You Be with Me Tonight?

will you be with me tonight
when the demons come?
all the doubts running like molten wax
from the wick of my heart, trimmed
too tightly by anxious hands...
holding me against the lost causes
I sold out for you and your eyes,
spinning webs that I can never cut,
never tear, never touch for fear
that you might one day awaken
and realize that there is someone
in this world besides yourself.

Votive

the cycle cuts both ways
and the haze that lays upon the sky
falls in cascades unafraid of your perceptions.
conceptions, missed and made, kissed and played
for a fool, held in continuous catalepsies.

the promise makes a mark.
stark realizations evoking amotations
in the mouths of children reaching for the golden apples,
sold and consumed in fists fitful and frail.
the sail of the horizon turns away, if only in the dimlight.

the riddle takes its toll.
soul food for the role we all play in the dance.
chances exchanged in dances made to execute a single turn.
and we burn. oh we burn with incandescent passions,
fashioned in the image of our gods, however we build them.

the memory remains to tell.
and we will share it when we dare again to feel something
less than the most that we toast our fall over, the wine
of wisdom running across tongues made numb with the spices
that twice as oft as not have burnt our lips for a draught of heaven.

The Frost of Ill-remembranced Things

sacred whims, foresworn this night,
we banked them in the dark
to hide from sight a blessed light
in which we shield our mark.

a print that hands and solemn bands
can not and never steal.
a kiss, amiss, and yet in bliss,
to, by this choosing, seal.

in autumn I did drop my plumes
and slowed to sullen pace,
and barely made the sheltered rooms
to sleep a winter's brace.

and comes the spring on powdered wing
to wake me from my grave,
to test the mettle of this thing
we fought and sought to save.

The Taste of Remembrance

you reminded me of memory.
not a memory.
but memory.

that twisted lift of something.
something. something caught
on the roof of my mouth
like peanut butter.

but it is a soft mystery
that wafted in on winds
I had not smelled
since midnight in Venice,
with the jasmine
and the dreams
that coiled in eddies of air
caught in the shadows
that melted into you.

true to your nature.
true to my hunger.

your shoulders bare to my touch.
your eyes closed to my thoughts.
and all else open and warm
and something like music.
something like music
when it comes upon you
suddenly, but beautifully,
like a lover at first waking.

and memory tasted a lot
like your lips.

The Patchwork Skirt of My Love

the sound of soft fingertips across the strings of a lute.
strumming the memories. humming the melody of life.
and I am lost in the possibilities of your presence,
pleasant, peasant prayers that lead to the summit
of the mountain in the distance, where legends reign.

kings cannot know this brandywine. princes pass perplexed.
and all the bishops seem ignorant of the nature of God
when their ignorance of the crux of creation is displayed,
paraded in the sudden dance of a smiling child by the fire.
and I am lost in the reverent reveries of this revelation.

play for me that melody, the one you tried to teach me,
you tried to reach me with when I despaired of lost love
and the angels and faeries all seemed annoying pinpoints
that pricked and sticked and stole the moment that was mine
and you came for me, barefoot and arrogant, like a poet.

and the fires swam into the sky and I, I was reborn.
torn to pieces and re-assembled like a patchwork skirt
to brush your bare legs in the summer heat and to defeat
the angry winds that would come down from the mountains,
mounting the horses of hoarfrost to charge your charms.

I live now, in more than just abstract recollections of a score
of forgetful lovers who would not give me second thought
were it not for the trinkets of my words they wear as bright badges
as they tell their tales of the pale blue moon of memory.
and they don't wear the patchwork skirt of my love. or play the lute.

TRANSCENDENCE

the heavens are in heat tonight
for this penitent, penetrative dream.

the iron lion stands astride memory.
mantichore wings of black lace fragments
of a leather lost to the weather of whim.
to him alone is there an accounting.

countdown.

grey skies to brown toxic fumes
as the hypergolic moments when
soul and intellect touch in the ceramic chamber
of a nautilus heart.

the skies scream aside in a fictional friction
of breath drawn out to thread like taffy
pulled too long.
an obit of an orbit, undecayed
as the patina colossus pulls free his lame heel
from the grounding earth
and raises high the last romantic verb.

liftoff.

and I am gone.
gone beyond imagination.
a consecration of madness
sold in gold and honeysuckle silver.
quicksilver slowed to sublimate
into a crystalline matrix of time.

farewell.
farewell.

but it is no longer my concern.
for I burn tonight in orbit no longer.
stronger than an epiphany
made construct in the shallows of an id.

Into the Grey

I can't imagine love
unless it is cast in the image of you.
Graven images of joy
and peace, telling me all that is true.
But you
have slipped into the grey.
And you
have nothing left to say.
And you
won't be coming back again.
And I
have forgotten what it was like when...
I can't imagine love.
I have lost my way, and all I can say
is that you are deity to me
after a long night, watching blackness melt away.
But you
have slipped into the grey.
And you
have nothing left to say.
And you
won't be coming back again.
And I
must live in violent silence 'til the end.

In the Morning I Will Be Gone

in the morning I will be gone.
but who says a night can be measured in hours,
the tender splendour of light at rest
when the zest and the best of the world
falls into small corners to be pressed together
like pages in a journal full of wildflowers.

in the morning I will be gone.
because that was the deal we sealed in wordless words
heard only by us in purely furtive looks,
nooks and crannies of our revelations filled
with all sorts of lies we tell ourselves
because the truth hurts too much, too much.

in the morning I will be gone.
and you will launder and press and fold
and put away the memories that seemed so important
when they were being made, fading to jade,
pages that never yellow as we never look at them
except in the darkest of nights.

in the morning I will be gone.
but who says a night can be measured in hours
the tender splendour of light at rest
when the zest and the best of the world
falls into small corners to be pressed together
like pages in a journal full of wildflowers.

I Will Come for Tea

I will come for tea, as promised,
to make certain you are well, in your exile,
hiding out from the complexities and vexities
that got in the way of who you wanted to be.

I will bring a small, lacquered box,
which I will take with me when I go,
leaving behind the gift of this year's visit, always there,
but never the same and something of a mystery.

I will come for tea, as promised,
and you will show me your garden, a source of pride
and life and the colours you draw upon to paint
and write and give us sight into the world you rule.

I will walk the cliffs with you, the sea crashing
with practiced rhythms that we will have to adapt to
if we are to speak with anything more than eyes
and the occasional touch to shoulder or wrist.

I will come for tea, as promised,
never making the offer I once made, for you know
it is still there, like a floorboard that creaks when stepped on
and never needs to be spoken of, unless you want to say "yes".

From the Parapet

the minstrel said
"the first cut is the deepest"
but I am not so sure...
as the only proven cure
for a broken heart
is to wrap it in swabs of clove
to desensitize the nerve.
and I will not surrender
my grandest passions
even to not remember
the feeling when the blade
hits the bone
and cuts through
to the marrow.

like last time.

and every time.

for the heart feeds or withers.
so let the candles be lit.
and the tapestries hung
and the windows opened
to let the night air
and the garden paths of stone
bear the tread
of the next fair woman
who will share the whole
who will bare her soul
who will dare control
the stallions of Apollo
as I brave the cliffs
in the name of love.

Love is an Howling Beast

love is an howling beast.
consumed by rage that cannot hate.
fate, sealing wax and clay and stone
o'er bone and blood and flesh.
yes, flesh, meshing in memory.
memories born of hope.
torn to grope
in darkness, when what you need
bleeds out in the gutters
as silence utters
a grave pronouncement.
a riot act, a solemn pact
stacked atop distant mountains
too far to see more than
featureless white.
I would peel back my own flesh
with raw fingertips
to know again the texture of her lips
the scent of her hips
and to not have as mocking memory
the trips to the well of her heart.
I am that grotesque statue
left in silent field
for future generations
to wonder on the purpose of.

Sisyphus and Prometheus

this is not a love poem.
for love does not lay upon me
like sweat and air
and the sour taste of rain.

it is a moment
captured like a firefly
and left in the jar
too long to survive.

but it is an honest thought
and it retains at least
the shape and substance
from whence it came.

pain. self-pity. loathing.
a world weariness like poison
driven in with careless needles
to steal what little remains.

Threnody for Times Now Past: 3/17/1979

the loom of doom had woven
us together...we who are anathema to reason,
the ending of a season of hope.
I would not be able to cope
if not for you, my dreams would be sterile and cracked.
the bags are packed.
I despise the coldness that wraps us in its cloak...
I choke back the lachrymal emissions...
our positions are self-revealing.
big boys do not cry...
but they can die.

the feast is done.
the beast has gone and left us...
so alone we listen to the breeze...
the thief flees and leaves us to measure the loss.
I can not. shall not.
dare not count this the end.
never was there such a friend.
call upon me. fall upon me in times of pain.
more remains than may be acknowledged in this moment.
the seed still lives.
but the shoots are now trimmed to encourage proper growth.

A Vile Attar

Deceit is a vile attar.
Avatars cut to the heel,
sealing the cryptic stonework
with words absurd and brittle.
Spittle trails, the banshee wails,
and the sails are torn apart.

A heart pulses equinox...
locks piqued with unsteady hands
demanding the ransom lost,
tossed aside in pride or rage.
Waging a war for its own sake,
taking the waking to die.

And I, I am still aware -
faring better than I thought.
What I have learned I will keep,
sleeping on a sea of dreams,
reams of the truth unpublished.
I am better than I thought.

More Than Flesh

Rome was an illusion, this time.
bleached walls and the smell of cinnamon
carried on my sleeve, leaving me a mirage
dissipating in the cooling light of evening.

I am reconciled to this, a virtue of my age,
a virtue of one who never counts love given
as a waste of a perfectly good present,
for the value is in the one who gives it freely.

the cold catalepsies do not return.
I have passed the third marker on my way
beyond the Pillars of Hercules and out and away.
the grey stain as a scar worn as a badge of honor.

to sail for the horizons, hands rough on the ropes
with which I steer these sails of patchwork dreams,
unseasoned no more, but aged and worn,
tempered by the sun and the breath of Aphrodite.

I smell the fragrance of freedom, a lie unwound,
but a moment's intoxication to be bartered
for a soft hand and a smile that touches
more than wind, more than lips, more than flesh.

Waiting for the Pentecost

there is nothing sadder than the persistent scent of your fading attar.
the sheets, no longer so warm and pampered by your frame, sorrowed.
but not as downcast as I am, clutching aroma'd memories to a scar
where once was a heart, fiercely pierced and glad to bleed unborrowed
emotions, potions imbibed in subtle sips not just to sample, but to prove
the leisure of the treasured pleasure to be measured in infinities.
a resurrection perhaps to be as prophesied in your eyes, to move
me to the transfigured instant of passion and purpose, or to disease
a soul already spread thin on wings of wax and stolen feathers.
as I am frail, so is the sun an inconstant lover, comfort in winter
and the furnace of the crucible of doubt in summer's span, never
more than less than welcomed according to the need of the lover.
and I have trusted skies too deeply to not regard the rose's kiss a true
friend before evidence of thorns is regarded in accepting the legacy of you.

Shroud

you are the shroud I shall be wrapped in
when my time is passed to speak for myself
and my words are twisted in wormspeak
for future generations to puzzle over.
"did he really love her?" they will ask
and I will have no way of replying
to correct misunderstandings caused,
as oft as naught, by your words and actions,
the shroud about my decaying legacy.

oh, to be spoken of in truth and not puffs
of pale smoke and pink meringue memories
that lay upon sheets long discarded to fade
like serenades of a lost love, echoing
only in the ears of those who heard them,
raw and true and through the bedroom walls
where we spoke them in inarticulate wonder.
I am bound for dust and ash and curiosities
that can never be resolved, even by death.

The Bottom of the Bottle

at the bottom of the bottle lay the final wishes.
irrecoverable, painfully arcane, buried in
regret and the ruby blue faceted glass, a prison
for what was once a man. now vivisected for whimsy
and whatever sustenance he surrendered too gladly,
madly shedding skin and sin for brittle reality
that was always just in the next pair of eyes that perceived
him, trapped in this lifeless state, waiting for the redemption
from his own regrets. forgiven of God, but not by man,
or woman, damned to be bound in a metaphoric maze
where love is a bandyword posturing children abuse
in their mad rush to be grown into a society
where grace is perfidy, power is abuse, and pretty
butterfly lies are best forgotten before the mourning.

Final Sunday

I am cast out.
orphaned.
left for dead by the side of a wide road
so that others can swerve
to miss my fading form.
nothing warm
comes from this.
another legacy of ashes
left on my tongue
the taste of dung
and vinegar
from an apple orchard
I had once considered
a sanctuary.

the colding feat.
I am incomplete
and competing for sustenance
is not in my nature.
I will drag myself
into the dark
that I may not offend
those for whom
pain
is too intimate.
and I will find
myself. unbroken
once I fit
all the pieces.

drinking stagnation.
the hunger unabated.
but I will bind my wounds.
plant fists to earth and roar.
sore in a thousand places.
it is good you do not
have to see me like this,
the tattered, battered man,
the orphan of Aphrodite.
but I will not change
my coat of arms.
I will still be a priest to your divinity.
and I will love you
every time I feel my hollow soul.

Bohemia

the wind is warm. formless and granular. the sand whips
the masts of the ships that never sailed, failed voyages
dry docked and stillborn, worn like a mason's hands.
the road is unmarked, lightly traveled, a pilgrim's afterthought.

the old man, blind in one eye, shades his brow and whispers
a solemn greeting, resplendent with time and tragedies.
"welcome to Bohemia", he rasps, dry lips spitting each word
like watermelon seeds at a long forgotten 4th of July party.

he rises. joints stiff and sore from the scores of times
he has risen out of common decency, even for those unworthy.
dignity and respect, reflected in a genuflecting smile,
warmer than the armor of the amourist, or something like it.

he motions you to sit and offers a scone or some warm tea.
"I remember what is important", he says, the mind still in motion.
the chairs are wooden, plain and solid, the paint scratched
and the table patched more than once out of necessities.

the wind continues to sing. And then he speaks, rapidly,
words unheard anywhere in the universe anytime before.
the poet's tongue dances though trances and transitions,
memories and good intentions, untended and befriended.

the wind fades, the sun sets, and the voice holds court,
sport of the mind, grinding the fist sized rubies to dust.
then blowing them away with a puff of breath, mocking death
and the stuff of riddles and religions, pigeons sacrificed.

the final syllables are what you came for, the final stanza.
you strain to catch your name in the arcane utterances.
it is in there, you are certain, the curtain cannot fall
without your acknowledgment in the dance of the decades.

you raise your eyes to thank him for his courtesy, despite
all the unrelieved grief and find him gone, leaving behind
only skin and bone and the riddle of manuscripts memorized
and now gone on a wind that resumes its mocking wail, outside.

from the book **Mythos:**

photo of and by Aysha Nasser, 2016

Prologue

Where the sun rises at the hands of my brother,
carried across the alien cinnamon sky, we won't die. No.
We shall be immortal, not born of mother,
but of the match observances of minstrels,
the lie of our creation obscured by the rabble as they fade
and pass into valleys of hungry legends,
sharp teeth to pierce the ripe skin but blunted
on the pink jade that we are shaped from, carved in perfect relief.

This is Olympus and Asgaard, the homes we ascend to,
Avalonian ripples in eternal seas we seize in cupped hands
to drink deep the draught of true nourishment,
it burns through the shadows of Plato and each nursery rhyme
that brands fleur de lis and Sumerian scripts no one can translate
as the tongues are forgotten, echoing in eternity
until the trouvere finds truer words that require
the weight of the penitentiary of the centuries to resolve mystery.

Artemis and Aphrodite mud wrestle for the fate of virtue
that Kinsey declared as smokescreens of burning hearts,
dampened cramps in the psyche of the tangled few
who cut through the Gordian hypercube to lube parts
for the sacrifice, nice memories if segregated
from bookends that carry the prologue and aftermath, integrated essence,
the presence of the granularity of the particular
odds and ends we collect in curious quests to find the purpose of our presence.

Woo

There is darkness that I bring to you and yet I bring lightness,
nonetheless, to protect you and to reflect you
in my words and life and daily press in the book
made of each fallen leaf and clover we take so we recall clarity and charity, belief
that love is regent against the fall. to lay with you each evening, wake
with you there, to smell your blessed essence on my hands and in your hair, to take
what I need, give tenfold to your presence. your heart is yours to tender, to share,
to hold in sacred trust until dust is the path and legacy. prepare a bed as adrift or to burn thrust
as is your desire, for the fire burns only when you breathe upon it,
heat given only by permission, turns kindling into inferno, the sweet
promise of emerged, encouraged touch of a flower blossoming bright to
bind and blind and find in manner such to redefine our passions, anew.

the madness of the elvish goddess

Some would flee, but it is not for me to judge the vow I take, I make
my way against the flow to find the path to her that may not be
a way that mortal men should take
if they would survive the sweet grind of the uncertainties that pierce
our flesh and thoughts. we are not set but we determine the outcome
in coeur rage and the passions fierce that burn us to the quick,
we whet our base appetites, overcome.

fusion

in the magma of your kisses I am melted as a stone,
to purify my essence, all my doubts to full atone
as a lost and blinded acolyte to worship past the veil
on an ocean of emotion to set course and set the sail
to touch soft against your beauty. to curve into your core.
to leave marks upon the corridors that you will let explore.

dread nemicorn

not a doppelganger for a past lover something, someone,
new and unique, like a dread nemicorn to consume the paisley powders
that dance on your breath as every small death
fills you with life
and a wicked will to curl like smoke around your tensioned, heated core to draw more
until I am hollowed out with hallowed shout to taste in haste and lay waste
to all your barriers that the beauty
that you share and surrender makes me remember
what poetry is supposed to taste like what dreams
are supposed to feel like what legends are supposed to be

arrogant tongue

where the merest brush of breath turns to kisses
the tip of an arrogant tongue takes tentative taste
then strokes
not unlike savoring an ice cream cone with hungry delight
but warm and sultry
as your fingers grip my hair and you grind against me urging me on
with feral sounds and the way your hips sway
when you feel the fire rise between the thighs
that alternate between trapping me tight
between them
or spreading wider
the better to invite me in
to feed for as long as I wish to your eventual
and repeated pleasure

sultry summer afternoon

sultry summer afternoon
when we generated our own heat sweet and substantial
in a sweltering shelter I took my time
finding the shadows
the welcoming darkness inside you
where you drew out my storm cooling yourself beneath me as you drank my sweet tea
of release
in ceaseless sips waiting for the night to lay a blanket on us
under which we would not sleep

on the edge of night

on the edge of night the edge of light the fleshes give up with a fight
and the bruised hearts illume with a radiation that speaks more than corners and curves

pure light
unbending and blending greens and grey and they play
against each other to make ruby-blue and white, white beyond your purest motives
where minds sublimate and fate
is our word for what we want more than anything else we've ever wanted

taunted by the calls of the priests in meaningless cants and chants
for that is sound, not electromagnetic waves that fiercely pierce even the ether
and neither of us is in a hurry
to scurry away from the pure light found only on the edge of night

ethereal eroticism

burn my flesh into a trace.
peel the diamonds from my face.
the passion, captured in light,
breaks the sorrows with delight in the wavelengths infinite,
beyond reds and greys, finite out of the necessity,
mocked and marked solemnity, merge surges inebriate
of which we now radiate unashamed in naked form initiating the warm.

Desire, dire and sacred

It would be a lie to deny
that what drew me first to you
was your unique, immortal beauty.
You possess grace and more than a little sensuality,
provocative and evocative woman-girl.

I have dreamt of you in wet, inhuman heat, feeling your legs
wrap about me, when I am inside you.
Whether I am tasting or penetrating you, you are Eros and ingenue,
draining my pain and feeding me joy.

To hold you to me and lose myself in hour upon hour of delight,
exploring you, worshipping you.
Expressing to you the passion you kindle in me like a bonfire.
Desire, dire and sacred.

petals touch

petals touch. lip to tip then kiss to dream,
laying truth along the seam
between your thighs.
veils that part. gentle touch to fire's bloom,
finding room to merge inside you
with no surprise.

Diving Deep

I would hold my breath a lifetime to reach the depths of your soul. No regret.
No doubt.
The patience of a lover committed to your beauty in all the turbulence
and mocking silence.
Aware of the risks.
Aware of the fury of the demons in the darkest silence.
Given to be taken and swallowed whole.
Out of passion and respect.

demarcation (pause)

the demarcation between the lemon meringue of your hair
and the pink meringues of your flesh
whipped into peaks by my attention and intention leaves me little room for error
and little time for wiser patience as you call me in.
in to the garden of your beauty. petals dew-swept where they wept in colder nights
but by the rights granted me
when you enchanted me
you do not sleep alone tonight if sleep is on the agenda
at all.
or just a feverish pause
when the claws you left in my back won't grow back
as quickly as I shall
and the sacrilege of your prayers murmured when I kissed your shoulders
on the path to enlightenments as to the color and the taste
of the fragrances
inherent in your blossoming and my release and surrender deep inside you
as requested and unprotested
throughout the night
that lasts beyond the Bavarian tests
of your passion and fashion for pleasure.

lightning and thunder

lightning and thunder take me under
to sunder flesh and soul
best to control me a part at a time turn on a dime
and make a meal of my zeal to not conceal
my passion for your insurrection
a real affection overturning and burning the ruins of years turning
into decades turned to dust but under the crust
the volcano god
is still evening the odds

pride and perfect kisses

brave and beautiful.
a majestic bird of mythology. you.
spreading your wings
to soar high above the binding grind of everyday care.
I will watch you
and watch over you as long as you allow making my bed
where you are keeping you warm when the night is cold
and finding a religion beside you
inside you
with pride and perfect kisses.

Persephone

night is but a state of mind I find
like sorrow or love
when the glove is threadbare we touch with fingertips
the heart set apart wait with expectations that will not be met
by anything less than the truth. removed from the currents adrift
a rift between what is what should have been what could have been
but for the tiniest of misspoken words heard with cautious ears
translated into pain
that the mourning comes to seal us without light without hope
not even a goodnight kiss from lips that never were except in exceptional dreams.

Xochiquetzal

your breath is intoxicating evidence that you are alive
and as it quickens it amplifies life to a sacred mystery
to be untangled as we tangle like writhing lithe liars
speaking the truth only with flesh and inner spirits
released in the task caskets of our transfigurations.
Veils sail away in a shower of flowers, butterflies
and the manifold marigolds strewn in your path.

ruby blue and true, blood floods and courses,
forces we cannot deny try as we might to fight the surrender,
pretender to a false immodesty. transcendent precedents
swept from the table as soon as we are able
to catch our breaths and affirm our deaths
in a celebration of a thickening taste we placed
like communion wafers of an intimate religion.

leave no stone unturned, our band and brand is burned
into the cracked and sacked altars stacked high in our inquiry,
our diet of wyrms wherein we throw down our theocricide
ride our preferred angels into the heavens
on until morning becomes another charade parade
of the pretense of civilization we shed last night.

Holle

there is a natural order
even in the most unnatural of things

like you like me

left behind, bereft of wisdom, we are the rich and the raptors
we steal hope and cope with the life before the afterlife as if it matters

like you like me

the benevolence of sufferings that drives, drives us like cattle into the shadows
to seek our desires in corpse lilies and the occasional penetrating rose sacraments of the fearless lovers

like you like me

Venus

the veneration of Venus, Aphrodite to the barbarians
who cannot pronounce the simple shibboleth,
religion and cult, mystery of the purging urges
that surge in wet and electric arcs that make stark
our most sacred vows and open us to desire.

fire, tongues of flame that lick us sick and slick
to better complete the intricate simplicities
of our measured pleasures. every inch
a phantom fathom that lowers us into a purgatorial pit from which
we can crawl out later, for we are here for the show

Bast

Cast your spell and I will pretend to fall under it.
But I am here for my own reasons, my own seasons
calling my whim to willful need to bleed my seed
as deep as you can survive as you summon life.
I will leave inside you more life than ten thousand spheres
brought to tears by the awareness of their sterility.

crystals crack and the gestures wrack limbs, lips,
and fingertips that slip through holes in the night
to weave the venom of our most virulent whispers,
blisters on the black wards you scored in fire
on the very stone I am touching even now,
against all your oracles and ordinances. the sky dances.

and we are still. catching breath.

Qetesh

awake, arouse, and slake the great hunger you burden me with
waiting for your revelation your consecration
in tenuous lips and grinding hips that meet and grind to throw sparks
and find the gem at the core of mere stone formed of the core of stars
and reawakened in the sacrifice of our solitude
in rude ecstasies

Saga

never less than friend, trusted and welcome in any season, for any reason.
an equal and a fitting sequel to the memories that are unworthy passion
you reflect upon, when life is waiting for us.

rowdy and refined, of merged or conflicted mind, we enjoy our adventures, delighted
to not have to walk these rocks and roads alone. we find wisdom in absurdity
and something epic, every day, to astonish us.

attar of the altar

in these darkened spaces,
traces of our other senses explore and implore,
soaring into atmospheres where tears
are lubricants and the watercolors
of our painted, sainted dreams.
traces of our faces that develop in silence when we express
with a language that existed before there were words.
cool sheets heated to warm us, form us
into a mythic beast of two hearts, parted only by the thinnest of excuses.

sin

I can sin with you from eight thousand miles away,
trading day for the familiar architecture of minutes after midnight
when we lay down our shame and blame only ourselves
for the roar of silent synergies, full lips and hips that grip
with a fervent hunger to be filled and fulfilled
in a chaos born of intent spent on pale idols that melted in the rain,
sandstone and salt that wasn't our fault we wanted to believe in

amomancies

words are shadows in the light of the sun, albedo neglected,
intentions reflected and perfected as I whisper dark delights
that you want to hear in the most irrational moments,
infinity and aleph,
the philosophy of the human heart and soul, filtered in blood
and the flood of subtle urges, urgent to be spent
on a street corner when the hunger is not honed
by honest consideration of hope and the rope
we hang ourselves from when we let others
tell us, sell us, on what they say we want. the religion of the gullible.
kiss me, again, when you are ready to share and care and dare
with a dervish passion, the taste of sweat on your skin,
secret words that will never be revealed as they are concealed
by the darkness, parked around the corner,
drawn like a patient smile of pleasure measured
against the legends of our amomancies and our desires.

lip service

you taste like jasmine. with a trace of cinnamon.
as I earn your earnest delight in slow hunger revealed
in between your taut thighs and grinding hips.
you sound like you like it when I know you really love it
but I let you underplay your hand so that I can kiss you into bliss.

shall I stand in the shadows

if you must hide me from the world
do so with the style of a princess or lady of the Court of Love,
Acquitanian legends, and do right by your desire, t
that I may serve my lady, in private counsels.
shall I stand in the shadows that, one day,
we shall be lovers in a mythology.
as well as in fact.

to serve the courtesan

the lights must be of the proper level of illumination.
the warmth of the chamber, pleasant to bare skin.
the scent of honeysuckle and plumeria present
in subtle seduction of one more sense,
not to violate the rose petals on the bed or the jasmine of her flesh.
tonight the courtesan pays her visit,
to lift my spirits with her bare feet dancing on stone and rich carpets.
her voice like starlight.
her laughter like sunshine.
her skin is the warm fabric of beauty textured to dreams.

amomancies call weave like smoke of incense through the air settling
in fragrant pools within our minds, binding
us to a common experience and intention, mention
of hearts and souls and the midnight magic she summons.
the illusion is that she serves me, but I am enthralled
held to her whims and the sway of her hips, her lips branding
my flesh with a fire and conspiring to take more
than just a whisper against sheets to summon
blithe and lithe spirits to dance in my imagination.

I will bind her in satin ribbons, red and black as to her mood,
make her food for thought and deeper hungers
we seek the limits of our rectitude and we intrude
in fantasies that perhaps should stay in our imaginations
but for the innocent curiosity of the meaning of our natures
nurtured in graceless ages to bend but not break.
cherished touch and the perished pains that we embrace
in our tentative temptations, born and borne and sworn as oaths
of a prescient purpose to draw nearer and dearer.

shared sacrament

in selfish, and yet shared, sacrament we vent our soft and feral needs
in deeds of friction and wet release for hours upon hours,
our powers merged and melted in unsheltered evidence of our desires,
fires bright and flesh set afire.
the test of truth.
I am in you, curving into your infrared the darkness that illuminates with heat,
sweet and sustained, pained by knowing
it is transient and it may be days or months
or never before I feel your brisance again.
so I surrender to the savour and the flavour of your lips
and hips as they eclipse
all sanity and vanity for the price of feeling,
feeling you embrace my face
and place rare sacraments of my seed within you.
all corners and curves consecrated. you are made holy
and laid claim to as I press aside your veils and share
these holy waters as proof against denial
of what we are and were and will strive to be.

vector

I provide the vector you provide the curve the iron of my entry
will bend to your every swerve you will swallow up me
and I will fill each nerve

the gentle glide of hands pressed against the smooth spiral of your emotions
as they feed you need you bleed you
for an extended moment's pleasure measure by measure touch by touch
such sensual light burning a tattoo
of invisible runes deep into you with every lap and kiss and penetrative trace
of fingertips as heralds to a deeper thrust into the puzzle box of your body
lips touching in every sense and tensions tightened and let in increasing
unceasing releasing wet and fevered
as you draw out my sacrifice exchanging passion for passion
as expression of earnest peace until the feral chaos of the next hungry consummation

solferino symphonies

a night, full of solferino symphonies. sweet and musky,
dusk made flesh then an intimacy of fearless lovers.
the legends are true and you understand your place in them
above any mere pantheon.
before there were gods, there were titans, greater than fate.
but even stone is thrown down by time and the self-serving betrayals
who covet a throne of bone and blood, flooding senses with relentless release.
making love until the darkness falls
then waking me with your insistent hunger. more than the animals,
less than the memories. the music of our very breaths
testing the acoustics of the cathedrals the altars
the hidden shrines, divine and delightful even
as they speak words of the inevitable as this moment's immortality is sealed
in heated oils and the spoils of pleasure.

flow

flow from the mountains, flow to the sea, time is a river of raging chaos.
lust and fear, the distant and the near. holy scriptures of beliefs disproven
or at least discarded when inconvenient. a night fit for a Bavarian king,
no ring but the filling is sweet and savoured
in labours laboured in a night without shadows where the glow of inferred infrared
lights the bed and the room, dispelling gloom in a solferino glow, going low,
then rising up and into a heaven awaited in a purgatory
they never taught in the catechism of false idols teaching their self-involved delusions
that nonetheless served their purpose as I flow into your delta in turbulent joy.

to speak of love in many ways

I know not what tomorrow brings to light as we are at length but a prophet's plot,
given to live, to be forgotten, right or wrong. The mysteries that we have got
and those that slipped away taunt and haunt us,
but these are dust, riddles of no laughter
as we reach with earnest hands for purpose
beyond the moment, for lovely answer
calming our doubts and pouts, then tender peace.
Such joy best between two antipodes
that reach a communed sense of true release
from the sad and mad, senseless urgencies resisted in harmonic affection
compelled to an higher pledge and passion.

compatibility

the truth of the solitude is that it is more unnatural
than any perversion, for we are made
to fit like cunningly cut jigsaw pieces. interlocking and measuring
against the overall picture of our vision of life. each curve and corner
complementing one then another
until a picture emerges and we step back
to see the big picture.

artist

in the medium of creation
you are a muse and yet far more.
you move my soul without an effort,
drawing out the radiant spore.

you do not need me to inspire you,
you have demons of your own, angels dark and incandescent about you,
ruby-blue in photic tone, driving dragons to distraction,
tearing saints and demons asunder. a soul, elemental,
to flash the light and crack the thunder.

I am grateful to have found you,
you confound me with your airs. mysteries in the histories imagined
you sustain me with sweet manna and dark tares.

where I kiss you is a sacrament

I will kiss your lips and wander, finding solace where I might, touching the miracle of your eyelids, the delicacy of your ears. the elegance of your neck, feeling your pulse, I shall not bite, for I want you alive, all of you, kisses to mark where fears might linger, in every thigh and finger, marking what I would by your grace,
make vows to gods whose names are lost in forgotten rituals
of the ardent races of lovers, finding good in the way you shudder
when every line is set and crossed. you can watch if you want,
or lay back and focus on the touch of my arrogant lips
on breast and hips, eclipsing propriety
to make my suit and refute your doubts as to just how much
I want you, more than a moment,
exposing my venerant idolatry as I take my fill,
making sacrament on every altar spread
with the offerings of you heart and flesh, each stone a lover's bed.

from the book **Bragi**

photo of and by Mariya Andriichuk, 2017

William F. DeVault QUINTESSENCE

Bragi bleeds

the serpent and the succubus are baring polished fang for you.
I caught the faintest glimmer of greylight
off their ruby-blue metal surfaces.
I heard the sheathes' whispering to me again
last night as I dreamed memory.

slow cuts the quickslitter that drives home venom angry and opaque.
take this phial and drink warm wine tonight
when they come for you, as I do.
no less breathes a riddle than I.
no more to dream the clocks' mockery.

pig iron and the myth of idolatry

John Henry was a fool
a slave who gave his life
for the notion that you are only a man
if you die trying to keep up
with the quotas and expectations
of the management class

holding you down
bleeding you dry
until your heart bursts
the hole still gets dug
the steel is still driven
the Mark II machine is brought in

songs will be sung
to your widow and orphans
maybe they'll make a monument
to your misplaced heroism
dying for another man's cause
is not the same as living

eclipse in Olympus

Apollonian indulgences
hoping Artemis leaves the party early
pretty pretty things dancing for smiles
and the hope to be spoken of later
when the minstrels show gratitude

the Gordian knot caught up in naught
but the illusion of the transience of life
this world is a single flicker of the strobe
and we disrobe to impress, undress
in the outer chambers and wait your turn

Hephaestus has his Aphrodite
although I doubt she is faithful, too many

shepherds and minstrels and demigods
playing the odds with a vessel of wine
and a line taught them by the stranger in the corner

infidelity

I should have stayed with you, remained faithful.
lived up to the idealistic ideal that was perhaps unreal
yet would have left a clearer legacy than caterwauling
and the stranger who believes what they will because
it is consistent with the mythology. sea serpents and such.
much is dangled, tangled, star-spangled as a banner
for an army that never marched anywhere but into Hell.
following the trace faces that were there for the rush
and the footnote in some distant collection of memories
hemorrhaging the rage, the coeur rage, the phage
of the page of the unamused muse when her totem
fades from prominence and is taken from the shelf
by the forces of history, mystery, and the scent of jasmine.

totemic

my heart was yours to use for a season
until you grow tired of it and forget
all the perfumed soft words sacrificed one
night when you had use of the fire I set
burning my manuscripts to split the night
before it had crushed you, rushed you away
from where you thought you wished to be, to light
bonfires of dreams to rise as oaths to pray
when all it was, in truth, was darkness' fear
to be bartered for warm lips and comfort
in the pretense never understood here
where I stood as collateral report
a calculated risk that my respect
that to fallen flesh I'd still genuflect.

the grief of Bragi and Apollo

it is the grief of Bragi and Apollo
that flowers wither and die.

ancient religions. the cure and curse of man.
passions personified, deified. made into words
that endure beyond the flesh and fluids
of our need to be merged with the divine.
nothing but the idols and temples
remain beyond the moment.

are there not yet goddesses who walk the night?
are there not yet whispers in the silent halls
that wend past my chamber and my tomb,
the womb of my immolation and resurrection?

it is the grief of Bragi and Apollo
that flowers wither and die.

so many broken chalices. so many shattered vows.
so many craven cannibals among the sacred cows.
and we are but the story. we are but the words.
we are made to burn and pass. we are. but not I.
what the blood cannot purchase, the soul consumes.
what the hunger strips from us is...everything.

show me the path. teach me the dance. make me yours.
there are so many parts of me yet salvageable.
there are so many parts of me that you would have use of
and that I would gladly give on an altar of madness.

it is the grief of Bragi and Apollo
that flowers wither and die.

I can, at a distance, with a word, with a dream or thought,
touch you in ways mortal flesh cannot and will not
for those gates are sealed against sentient degrees
of heat and seduction. we give what we can, hollow.

right there

stop right there. consider not only the moment
but the infinite cascade you invite with every action
and fraction of thoughts
conveyed in unreliable words

words are zephyrs and bricks
and sticks you use to poke awake
the sleeping dragons
or beat them into submission or retreat.

I can see and have described
colours you cannot imagine
and the quantum chance you may
catch me pleasantly or unpleasantly by surprise.

evolution

I will yet evolve. but I am what I am.
potentials and past imperfect and realized
at levels of granularity that you, and even I,
shall never comprehend. I won't defend myself.
poets take body blows and butterfly knives
straight in and to full effects.
you cannot make a silk purse
from this sow's ear, but near as I can tell
you have enough purses already.

we are social creatures

we are social creatures, features that fulfill us do not come from solitude
but in finding where the cut cardboard curves best complete the image.
the self-indulgence we pass off as proper reflection is a rejection
of our best fates and forms, the warm norms of trust and peace
in the release of our worst precognitions and errant arrogances.
understand what you can, accept the rest, and test your best bets
we place against shallow and fallow standards sold like dry lamps
that do not give light or heat or hope once the market closes
and we are left with the indifferent differences between myth and madness.

djinn

if I poured smoke to encase erase replace the ordinary
that grinds us down with the fantasies you dream of

would you have the courage to make a triptych
of the diptych you gave me as a present in the past
where so much was left unresolved.

I want to answer every curiosity you ever dared asked
and help you find the courage to ask more.
I want to swirl in eddies of mist that have kissed
the faces of every prayer you would dare
give upon unaltered altars, as an agent of change
often unrecognized after over the horizon
and never to be seen in constellations again.

William F. DeVault   QUINTESSENCE

Bragi to Freya, on his deathbed

I am not blind to the beauty
but like a paralyzed man
his bed a prison
unable to touch or taste or smell
only those things brought to him
or that, by accident, slip though the walls
of glass and steel and watchful eyes
that institutionalize lies
to their own ends.
the sterility befriends
those whose clothes tell a tale of wanderlust
in worn soles and frayed hems and dust,
dust of a thousand roads
some walked to the horizon
some merely tested with timid toes
like an unfamiliar water pool at dawn,
yawning a frigid maw to pull you in
and cramp body and soul.

I am not blind to the beauty
but bound to it.
The sound of it is like music to a deaf man
who can perceive the bass line as it shakes
the snakes from the foundations of a world
made of a necessity, a necessary doubt
of things spoken with too much conviction,
words used as truncheons
to beat down relevant inconveniences.
The luxury of truth is something few afford
in the discordant umbilical left to hang,
to dangle at an angle on the edge of cliffs
we once leapt from, unafraid of the consequences
of gravity and the pursuit of knowledge.
I can see it, eyes open or closed,
limbs and lips languid or posed
like posturing candidates for a title
I am not sure I would or should award again.

William F. DeVault   QUINTESSENCE

I am not blind to the beauty.
I am not deaf to the music.
I am not cold to your touch.
I am not tongue-numb to your taste.
I am not unaware of your perfume
as you enter this room
and leave a telltale marker to be followed
into Elysium, if I am willing to rise
from my chosen catalepsy
and wear again the patchwork pelts
and the mark of my station and office
to follow where I swore I would go
when the word was given in silent mouthing
from across the room but in plainsight,
for I am not blind to the beauty
as I plant my fists in the stones
and press upward with aching muscles
to fulfill that which is ordained of me.

bonfire

the fire crackles in staccato code
secret words unheard since creation
as what once were trees towering overhead
and providing rest and shelter
are consumed to leave ash and memory.

in the moment they are generous and luminous
the dancing flames reveal the names
of everyone we once loved who is now
ash and memory and so much past refractions
of futures we once had never imagined.

and a dove

plainsong and the stench of regret, sweat as baptism,
the schism spreads like a sickly grey pollen, fallen
angels moult feathers for leathers and beat the wind
into submission. I will wait for you to sober up,
as into your cups is not the same as into me.

what for you may be a habit or hobby is to me religion
with you as the highest priestess, if not an avatar
of a goddess drawn near by the promise of worship
and the words to make a scripture for future generations,
hungry to know what was not defiled in this graceless age.

what I am what I offer what I am becoming under pressures
that warm and deform any and all who even stand near
enough to stuff themselves on the fragrant flagrant essence
consuming us as it nourishes us. as it should be.
a faith in more than self. a sanctifying kiss and coit.

learning of the death of a well-regarded ex-lover

you called my name on your deathbed and I was not there.
those in attendance did not hear, or did not care, or did not know
a history you had left in mystery as if of Diogenes, naked revels
in a passing sense of security and freedom where life was live
and meant to be swallowed whole. peyote and mescaline.
hallucinogenic revelations. the overpowering flower of your garden,
tended, mended, ascended with unconditional enthusiasm.

it would have been my wish and will to be there for you,
but I do not manipulate to consecrate, accepting free will
with the attitude of a deity choosing to embrace it as righteous.
when the word reaches me, if ever, of your passing…
I will be lost in the distant but persistent reveries you invoke,
speaking not of you to pagan pretenders who have surrendered
their place at the altar for less arduous purposes and paths.

feigning

feigning sleep when all I could do
was lay awake and dream of you.
your perfect flesh a canvas of desire
a poetry of warm presence, eloquent
and true. beautiful and mesmerizing.
not yet. maybe never. but dreams
are the currency of lovers at night.

evil

evil is a slippery thing, flesh fresh from the shower
before we apply powder to reveal the fingerprints
hints of what really happened
while we were lying to ourselves
on a bed of roses poses and suppositions
reclining and seemingly upright
to man (or woman) the barricades
against the barbarians of the week

the moment

like a lover
you are here
now
for your own reasons
obvious to no one
not even yourself
seeking revelation and penetration
into a merged state of being
something other than
stuck in the sucking muck
of five minutes ago

borders

I don't want to steal your freedom
but from time to time
be granted permission
to cross your borders
lingering
and sometimes
sometimes
watching the sunset
then being allowed to spend the night

chasing Apollo

gears and strings and waxwork wings
the engines roar with Promethean fury
the sky splits open against its will
as we arc to the West, chasing Apollo
back to where he tries to hide and slip past
our watchful eyes and lies, behind us
beginning again the ancient journey
we can only frailty imitate and wait
for maybe an afterlife in which we are
part of the chariot and not just staring skyward

raku: 1

porous clay to hold the graceful tea we share
in ceremonies that merely mime our passion.
fashioned by the hands of artisans and gods
to be durable and beautiful and of a purpose
incidental to the actual consumption of life
infused into water and leaves that grieves
then giggles as it contemplates the transition
from one form into another. like my mother
and my father and all the ephemeral darlings
that form constellations against the echoes
of the big bang that may have happened
infinite times before in the quantum foam
that drives us home after an unexceptional party

raku: 2

the most perfect gemstones are most memorable
when they are not perfect.
when flaws catch the light and render us awestruck
with the dancing fire and lightning
your flaws are your perfection, an insurrection
against the ordinary sameness
rendering reds and green and golds to grey
before it fades away to nothing

raku: 3

you must come to me of your own accord. not lured or bought or caught
in the webworks of my words, delicate, near irresistible,
or I will find myself in a moral conundrum where free will
and arch romance are at loggerheads and religion of desire
is thrown down as a clay pot to shatter on stony floors, the shards
only mocking token of what it was, broken like a promise
made in silent prayer to earnest deity, hamstrung on principle
making an impossible resolution in a logic trap
snapping shut at the most inopportune times as intellect breaks
against all the minstrel's magics to leave us cloistered in a cage
of our own best intentions and inventions, dark and thirsting dry
as the countenance of faith is beguiling and yet unsmiling.

raku: 4

in remembering you I forget myself
which may be the most blessed gift I will find
cast in ceramic madness to calculate
numbers that even Cantor would have thought mad
as I had it all then in elliptic orbit and obit
I spun so far away as to break the pull
of the solace of all the gods and goddesses of light

raku: 5

cast off blast off fast off the mark the court and spark
barking mad parking bad in the tow away zone
where we hone our peculiarities to an edge
to wedge to ledge our legends on the top
and stop to hop out and down to drown

raku: 6

in the season of the apple harvest I remember you, the unknown goddess
yet unrevealed although not concealed, a field of grasses in a photo
that was to be our announcement of our challenge to the world and time
but the wind blew and your tumbleweed toes made short work as flows
the sinister streams of yesterdays into tomorrows, leaving a present unopened
a riddle for the ages wages war on certainty and promises abandoned

raku: 7

every man or woman forges their own chains. alloys of memory and belief.
casting stones and casting the runes while whistling tunes without lyrics.
a drink of water. a sideways glance. the flavour of sunshine, divine
intervention and invention. pretensions and doubts. a fallen leaf
displaying evidence of the previous Spring. coiled steel with a ruby blue luster
a bluster of politicians and blasphemous preachers. poets: the weavers
of memory and moments outside of the present bound in soundless groans
while everyone is looking for a Messiah. or at least a good fuck.

Pyewacket

the simplest things hold no fascination, for in complexity is allure.
the pure spectacle of colored bits of broken glass in the kaleidoscope.
there are no one-petalled flowers, no night sky without dark pocks
against which the infinite incandescences leave their sparkling marks
to compel us to consider the splendid diversity of life and be sure
that a song made of one note, with no harmony, in which the trope
of mud against mockingbirds invokes, evokes, provokes the rocks
to sing plainsong. we are drawn to the friction, the fiction, the sparks
that come from conflict and a slightly askew smile that speaks of mysteries
to be constant against our consternation. immolations in the winter
of our most baffling boredoms and encapsulations of a craven raven
with but a single word we've heard, revealing nothing but our cowardice.
there are no saints found in the salt flats, no evil more than grey histories
filled to the shallows with ancient bones that will crack and splinter.
that equip us for naught but mediocrity and madness, our deities graven
by our own hands from balsa and excuses to the muses that we miss.
here is my praise for the complicated woman, for she is human and true
and made in the image of a God who carved all seasons and reasons
that we may burn or freeze, that made daisies and diseases, light and dark,
a kiss and a slap, to communicate the great spectrum that is more than seven,
more than false taxonomies put in place to grant barriers between green and blue.
the seams in my dreams make room for more climate than one season
to revel in diversities found in musics of infinite cultures, ornate and stark,
redefining, in the higher moments, the very essences of hell and heaven.

I do not chase the wind

I do not chase the wind
for it cannot be caught
and after I have fought
my way to the mountaintop
there would be no way to go
but down.

I do not chase the wind
for dreams are for their time
and I am wise, if past my prime,
and know how not to make an ass
of myself by thinking above the waist
sometimes.

I do not chase the wind
for it is but a metaphor
or five or six for the war
between the soul and the flesh
damned to fail and wail at rainbows
"Not fair!"

I do not chase the wind
for it would not be fair,
although if I would dare,
she might find me swift of foot,
carrying my golden apples of
poetry.

Walsingham in Padua

I have given my word.
Strange word, word.
It carries itself and more, boring eyes in the back of the skull
when you are full of your own definitions of honor.

It is said there is no use
in worrying about the water
when you are dying of thirst and you find it, bubbling up pure,
cold and with the slight air of the center of the Earth.

I have lingered enough,
bare feet calloused by pain,
denying myself and my desires. The fires a test of the metal
that is at its best zested by a kiss extended into madness.

I have broken with the past,
giving up more than you know,
accepting a new commission, a new purpose, head bowed
in humility that belies my arrogance and my skills.

You asked for me by name.
I am called back into service
of a distant liege who may keep me in foreign lands for a time
before acknowledging me at court, welcoming me home.

But I am grateful and ready.
I have counted the petals of the lotus.
I have tested the metal of my blade and my pen, obeying
the rituals that may seem arcane to you, but define me.

I will serve you until I fall.
I will not swerve or lose nerve
even if left, like Walsingham in Padua, to await the time
when all is to be revealed, I will stay true to my vows.

in the hall of mirrors: twenty

the apocalypse drips vinegar in the eyes of a bound god,
fallen from grace and tasting the acid of his failures.
impure, unsure and with no cure in sight for his blight,
he rattles chains and leaves stains of his own blood
to mark his presence and predicament. Phaeton's coursers shod
with dogmatic memory, bent and spent and sent on adventures
to buy back that which was given away on a misbegotten night,
the orchard of golden apples swept away in a flood
that orchestrates the fate of us all, our natures rebelling
against our wisdom, which is learned from burned fingers
that lingered too long, too close, to the heat of sweetness
that drew us in to a light in the hall of mirrors, mirage
and smoke dissipated by our own intemperate hastes, telling
more about the ballistic trajectory of our flesh we express
in words that curdle in the face of facades and badinage.
we stand as pillars of life and light, until the inevitable felling.

Erato beats her children

Erato beats her children,
Bragi takes to drink.
And within the dragon's den
I don't know what to think.

The shadows are upon me.
They smile in black and red.
There is no solace left to me
not even in my bed.

Erato beats her children,
Bragi takes to drink.
And within the dragon's den
I don't know what to think.

The knight, once white, is greying.
Tarnish takes its toll.
And hungry critters, preying,
find their victuals in my soul.

Erato beats her children,
Bragi takes to drink.
And within the dragon's den
I don't know what to think.

Calliope and Karnak.
A leprosy abounds,
more final than a heart attack,
and full of silent sounds.

Erato beats her children,
Bragi takes to drink.
And within the dragon's den
I don't know what to think.

the rise of Bragi

the kissed thistle parted and the voyage was started
on running feet, sweet with desire and a fire like light,
bright and weightless, the fates stated their objections
and we laughed, laughed like children at the wind.
but I have risen, and seen the flavour of the sky.
I have risen, and given my favour to deny
that I have not the hand to handle this curve
and much as I serve at your pleasure, it is wrong
to bind a god to an uncertainty, so resolve me.
once, and for all time, speak truth, even small words
have cured the greatest night of ignorance and doubt,
shouting truths does not make them lies, paper
sometimes is just a place we thought we'd been
and I have miles to travel to the end of the day.
join me. or, if not up to the journey, be on your way.
I walk with the serpents and the angels.

romantique

I touch you within a light, consumed and consummated
in a divinity relegated to a cliché wrapped in an enigma.
bitter herbs of a passed over past, the angel of life awakes,
taking me to a new evocation of demons as I reach within you
with etheric hands, unwinding like funeral shrouds to touch
the dead skins of trophies of fading dawns reborn and reborne
to the Suttee pyres where the survivor is expected to die
with the dead. and I said your name, the way you like to hear it,
with honest passion and a promise of healing tears to come.
and they emerge from an unexpected quarter to flood senses
already overcome with a truth that at very least, I shall never
relinquish to false memory for the purpose of the mocked dead.

Sigyn for my sins

there is no Sigyn for my sins.
none to catch the venom
that I have brought on myself,
the Earth, itself, shaking,
nonetheless,
from the agony of punishment.

the is no Sigyn for my sins.
no free will to defy the gods
out of pity and out of love.
better still, in love,
but the illusions persist.
like Gilda, I do not survive the night.

there is no Sigyn for my sins.
I have borrowed the chains
of Promethean glory, but am judged
unworthy to bring the fire.
for my sins I am outcast and exile.
the inexorable venom, my legacy.

Brutus: Act One

This diseased horizon. No smooth line to define
the necessity of good and evil, merely expediency
and the illusion of honor. The eyes of the prophet,
taken like Cicero's tongue, in outrage and revenge.

I walk this bloody parapet, stains visible to me, alone.
Asking gods and goddesses that are now trivia
to those who have not yet the bark of many winters
to allow them to measure the relevance of sin.

The coals flicker, but never die, sustained by will
and made merry in a sideshow feast of jeremiads,
everyone weeping until the clowns and jugglers return
in the next act, to sweep clean the inconvenient emotions.

Every stone speaks a story that I am deaf to hear.
Every story was important when it was a moment
in a day on a life that fell to those who lived it,
making the same half-aware sentiences of the world.

The honorable are played by the ignorant, who think
the upper hand is something of an higher order
of evolution. But it is the last poet standing
who determines the legacy, as words stick wicked.

I have no use for the bartered truths that get us
through the day and on our way to our next abomination.
I have given up my ambitions to serve an ambiguity
with the faith best held for the temple mysteries.

Hephaestus to Aphrodite

You are beautiful.
I, deformed.
A god, no doubt, but not one
that they burn fragrant oils
to gather the favour of.
I am unworthy of you,
unworthy of your love.
It burns within me, this passion,
and yet it burns before me
that for all bonds and bindings
you will never really love me.
Just the idea of me.
The lame god, in the forge of souls,
hammering shape to metals
I have drawn out of lifeless stone.

You are beautiful.
I, deformed.
Cyrano suffered thus, and ultimately
it cost him the woman he loved,
who would have loved him back,
I suspect (ask Apollo, he would know).
But he was man and she, woman,
we burn at a higher degree,
our passions set fire to the skies
and people run and scream and dream
that their hearts could survive such heat.
But they are not that sturdy.
You seek balance in my malformations.
You laugh and smile and feign passions
beyond the novelty of my hideous countenance.

You are beautiful.
I, deformed.
For all your beautiful words and soft touches,
I know what and who I am. I know the smell
of burning sulphur under my nails and know
that my kisses are that of a brute, a thing.
Not a god, which is what you deserve.
I am twisted and I know my place.
Those things which I craft, that is what is sought
by those who follow the twisting labyrinth
into the hot bowels of the Earth to find me.
Lovely ornaments of silver and alloys I alone
can make and master, for I am Hephaestus.
But that does not make me beautiful.
That does not make me worthy of a goddess.

William F. DeVault   QUINTESSENCE

Aphrodite

Goddess of the Chaotic Erotic!
queen of fantasies and flagrant fragrant passions.
beauty personified, like you, irresistible.
I surrender my essence, blessed Hephaestus,
a mere craftsman in presence of the divine,
beauty personified, like you, irresistible.

Athena

choices made, wisdom incarnate. understanding.
the power of knowledge and the knowledge of power.
what next is necessary and what are the wagers
and the likely outcomes. not omniscient,
but close enough to drive her forces to victory.
the excellence of superiority, found in reason.

Hera

Jealous wife. keeper of the hearth and home.
peer plotter to the most clever, to balance the scales
of fate that matched her with an incorrigible man-child,
who thinks that rage is power and plays his game
in seductions, reducing his presence to an archetype,
unworthy of the crown, stolen from his father.

Artemis

Mistress of the Hunt, bearer and healer of disease.
the cruel reality of nature personified, implacable.
doing what she, by nature, feels will please
her hungry heart and nature. fate's most able
agent of cruelty, but not of malice or intent,
for she is not judging those on whom her wrath is spent.

Demeter

Weep for your daughter, gentle Demeter.
Weep that she is stolen away, to dwell in darkness.
Rejoice in her return, but burn the fields in mourning
when she spends her seasons in the halls
of her most plutonic husband. Weep while nature sleeps.
How the very seasons are affected by your heart!

Dionysia

I think the god of wine and wild revels should not be a man
for what can a man know of the release through transcendence
that women do not already know and show us in seductions.
from the gardens to the Anthesterian mysteries. histories
of the race show us that women lead the parade and charade
when pleasure is measured off the scale through the night.

The Muses

Not the bastardized nine, but the true trinity of the Muses.
Aeode, the muse of song, whose voice and words flowed
like honey from the tight core of the world's divinity.
Melete, practice, to perfect the role and recitations,
to find nuance in the perfecting of passions expressed.
Mneme, from whom memory is personified,
the voice and repetitions granting immortality.
You are personified in these three, my love,
drawing out from me, and their goddess cousins
what of me is nothing less than my last, true religion,
in finding my theology in your arms and heart.

what remains of the street

Mitch is a bitch and she lives on the street down from her parents
off the grid a kid skidding closer to the edge where the sedge has withered
and the victim of her merciless mercies is her
as
the problem isn't with her but the forces that shape her
that rape her
that steal her sense of self-worth
daughter of the Earth told she is worth less than nothing
neon peon pain.
Wrong hair wrong eyes fat thighs and last year's nail color.
The hardest things are the most brittle
spittle is spat
blending with the street covered in rain and pain and stains.
Running into the gutter.

feeding the wolf

probably a mistake to step away. way away.
hiding in the open. missing kisses as a currency
of self-expression. words are immortal.
immortality is oversold.
the long, slow, inexorable drip
slipping into the riptide of torn emotions.
lying lovers covering their sins with my mantle
because I volunteered the veneer of my virtue
like some goddamn Galahad when all along
I know I am far from the paladin, the holy crusader,
fully cognizant of my flaws, the laws of man and god
that I have looked the other way on,
but in the isolation there is a vague reassurance
that I am still far from the nosferatu's dream
life can proceed
even if I have less time to capture
a muse to be my Sigyn
my Idun or any of a thousand
mythological or jungle beasts
that feast on nostalgia and notoriety
while I, I take my fill of models and mold,
the wolf takes cold showers
powered by perverse pride
in the ability to say no.

Hetaeron

I am known by many names.
Some names. Some sobriquets.
Some epithets of those unaware
of the many moving parts
in the truths they think they know.

In the West I am Hetaeron.
In the East the Amomancer,
the priest of passion. To myself
I answer to no name, for to do so
would bind me to the spirit of it.

In the North I bring the fires,
in the South I quench desires.
In lands far and uncertain,
I am called by whatever badge
that I will find on lovers' lips.

For the moment, I am content
to warm myself here, out of the darkness,
and wait for the songs to return,
burning my feet to walk again on paths
I had not realized until I heard the voice.

when the morning never comes

when the light is ever absent and the morning never comes.
when the silence is oppressive, not even distant drums
to mark the rallying of the faithful, the courage of the few
anew who pick up the banner of the purpose to the view
more than merely selfish, shallow dreams of centuries
fallen far too fast to justify the feasting of furies
surrendered to the pretense of virtue in expediency.
bound to madness and the sorrowed illusion of the free.

collision with the morning star

captured in slowly deteriorating orbit
of your Venusian plains
the hellish acid of your atmosphere
will burn brighter as I descend
in final fall to be consumed
doomed
by having been captured by your nature
to draw me in and spin me to
a cataclysmic finish
a sound that tears apart the ground and sky
as I am absorbed into you.

the aftermath of a passing flirtation
not oblivion
but the witness of those creatures
who saw my descent
and wondered at the nature of my origin
as my constituent elements become part
of the hard, sulfurous heart
forming the sphere of legends of light
love
and the scrimshaw of my fragments
that, even unobserved, are proof I once was.

Midnight and the heat rises

and all the lovers danced for dreams that never were to be.

in intricate and heartfelt sways beneath the elder tree
they worshipped with their mysteries they worshipped with their prayers
they worshipped through their histories retold in minstrels' airs.

and all the lovers danced for dreams that never were to be.

both Heloise and Abelard retained their lust to see
their paramour and more took up in currents to be caught
on colding sheets where feral heats turn all that is to naught.

and all the lovers danced for dreams that never were to be.

penitent and patient. penetrative, native to me
when I am immolated by your craving and desire
to sacrifice my seed and need into your greedy fire.

and all the lovers danced for dreams that never were to be.

I am the serpent

Coiling around you, my arms entangling your elegant legs.
My tongue, tasting the air and more, flickering as a trademark
An archetypal lover seeking to derive sustenance
This is not Eden, this is not Canaan, and not Megiddo.
I am but a humble serpent, asking the subtle questions
That will loosen your resistance and make you realize that
Taking the offered fruit of the tree of knowledge and pleasure
In your warm and not-unwilling hands and taste it between lips
Of every latitude and attitude to find and grind
Awakening you to your nakedness, as did I to sigh
And lie and die many times tonight to be reborn with you
As we become a cautionary tale for new religions.

Moral sentience

Moral sentience: the ability to know what is right and what is wrong.
There is more to good and evil than not doing one or the other,
Smothering ourselves in codes of conduct that teach nothing
But the rote memorization of steps to take and to avoid.
The kata of movement, square dancing in the darkness.
Precision maneuvers that accomplish nothing unless the action
Is more important than the intent or the passion, fashioned
Of smoke and shadows and mirrors and memory, anecdotes
That coat us in a sand-encrusted lubricant the tear us
And leaving little doubt but that we are worn down and away.

Little secrets

Tell me all your little secrets
The one you fear
The ones you love
Tell me all your little secrets
So that when I tell you mine
I will not feel too vulnerable
And if you don't want to
Tell me all your little secrets
That's okay as sometimes
People have buried their pain
So deeply that it is impossible
To recall on what exact shelf
You left that particular journal
Because nothing is ever really
Lost, merely misplaced.

The sabotage of gods

the gods sabotage themselves.
tired of being different
in a world where mediocrity
is prized above all else.
I have seen your radiance
as you shade and jade it,
pretending to be nothing,
pretending to be grey remnants.
it is difficult to be deific.
painful to rise above the muck.
we are our most comfortable
when we are nothing extraordinary.
it is easier that way, that path
of fieldstone and failure.
the allure of artificial urgency.
the gods sabotage themselves.

falling into darkness

it is only in the light that we learn what is that's right
and learn what we must fight against at night
the darkness and the black within us, pulling back
against all hope and dreams of peace, we stack
our paltry chips and dip our hands in holy water
for a gamble and a prayer we swore we'd never again utter
but here we are at equinox, slipping from the dream,
falling into darkness, with an ancient, echoed scream
that reflects off into nothing, there's no angel on the way,
the fall is all that matters. it is alone we pay
the price of our perditions and the sum of all our pain
laid against us on the jagged stones to pull a crimson stain
and deposit us as broken forms, a warning to be made
to the fools who would repeat the path in lover's foul charade

DFW

on the stones of our temptation I lay as shattered glass
fallen from a height, thrown down by my own gilt guilt, blood spilled
as sign of divine consideration, martyrs pass
in solemn procession of bowed heads and prophets killed
because the rabble did not care for honest message
delivered in appropriate judgement upon them
when they did not wish to see the truth their doom presage
in unsubtle words against subtle sham omens, gem,
bone, lots cast to disavow responsibility
for the actions we take, the vows we break, as we make
our own validations against our virtues, fealty
to our own justifications, our dreams come to wake
and mesmerize us with seven powers we deny
ever influenced us, we live in every lie.

Qoheleth

One day the very sound of my footsteps, so loud in your ears,
shall have faded and I will be an easily dismissed memory,
practically an abstraction, a fraction of a moment's thought.

Tales of my existence shall be bought and sold in manners
we have not yet considered, bound as we are to technologies
that sit before us and bore us waiting for the next big thing.

Someone will say they once met me, and others will pretend
that I am just a story made up to teach lessons to children,
plastic as their dreams are, plastic as their hearts and minds.

I will have been, as my writing these words here and now prove,
but my relevancy will be a question, for love and hope may pass
from the emotional vocabulary of mortals, the words lost.

My words will outlast this generation, and many more to come,
numb to their own vanities as in Qoheleth's distant teachings,
but truth endures, sure, pure, and to cure the follies that follow.

antiquated

the faint whiff of copper in my night sweats remind me
that I am not so young or fit as I once was.

but I am not ready to quit this world
and dive into the next level of existence.

I am still trying to tie up the loose ends
of a hydra born with Gordian DNA before I away.

the inconvenience of death is the loss of ability
to make for changes in this world, so I write.

love letters to the human race, laced with irony
and humility and arrogance and desperate hope.

beyond me

every day I wrestle with my conscience
seeking to draw out the poisons that I injected
with words and deeds I thought were needs
or at least natural reflex and instinct.
the war still rages within me
the evil and the divine, the point
by point
by point
debate between he who is locked in a cage
(but not allowed to die for I need his vigor
and his feral fantasies
to keep me appreciative
of the beauty and bounty of a world
that slowly fades from my grasp)
and the construct
the golem
(fashioned by my hands from unchaste earth
and animated by cognitive therapy
passing for prayer)
to serve as evidence of the art of the effort
to make of us more than just another
failed experiment
in the garden of madness and regret.

contemplative seduction

sit with me. we don't need to speak. a furtive glance or touch
communicates more than most words, and are heard completely.
touch me when you are ready. I will not recoil. but I want you
to be as content in all that happens, that it was by your will.
I have lived long enough to know the essence of joy is free will.
teach me the language of your touch, your eyes, how you breathe.
inhale me. close your eyes and see the shadows on your soul,
thrown by the illumination of my fire, dancing far enough away
that you are unburnt by it. but the light is there. see your presence
as interpreted by my impressions, then steer my fantasies.

surreality

I will not know the taste of the wind as it blows across the grass in Harmony Grove
ever again. Time passes and memories that are indelible still come distant.
Insistent resistance to the changes life arranges. Absent friends and family
who are little more than two dimensional images and names on Arnettsville stones.
Grief is not a relief for it relieves nothing, saline rain that stains aging skin grown thin
waiting for the worms that will be denied their feast when I am released by seal
and modern chemistry. Sarcophagus or urn. Everyone takes their turn to learn
what waits beyond the veil. Memory is the curse of those who care, heir
to a fractured throne and boneyard politics, ridicule and the tools of sepulture.

what dark magicks

spark spark spark spark
the tinder catches. then the kindling.
spindling tongues of flame climb
in defiance of gravity and the disingenuous promise of earth.
spark spark spark spark
whim becomes thought then dream.
plans made and actions accomplished.
the moment and the aftermath flow like thick dark blood.
spark spark spark spark
prayers and spells, amomancies and necromancies.
stolen breath. summoned death. the deceits of the prestige.
look away before the spark catches you unaware.

the blood of Kvasir

drink deep, even sleep will not still your mind
once you have taken in my mead. you feed
and then you feed others. sisters, brothers,
the children of mortals who never bleed
to so worthy of a purpose but that
heroes are woven of all the whispers
as the cithara draws the venom spat
by wicked serpents and pale visitors
whose keening wail chills your blood, faeries
that walk through walls and down halls forgotten
by all but skalds and trouveres, memories
weaponized to break the will of Wotan,
amomancies in Aphrodite's bed
where, tonight, I will lay her and my head.

About the Author

William F. DeVault has, in his creative run (so far) amassed tens of thousands of poems (and those are just the ones that passed first reading). He has published over 20 books, received his unfair share of sobriquets, and performed his poetry all over the continental United States. He has read in churches, bars, parks, schools, libraries, and brothels.

Married twice, divorced twice, but still the romantic optimist, he has fathered three children in whom he is well pleased, and mentored dozens of poets. He founded and lead the Romantic and Erotic Poetry Group for America Online, and that service's Passionate Craft poetry workshop.

He was named the **Romantic Poet of the Internet** by Yahoo in 1996 and the **US National Beat Poet Laureate** by the National Beat Poetry Foundation for 2017-2018. Many consider him the Poet Laureate of the Internet for his presence and pioneering use of the internet during and even before the mid-1990's.

Acknowledgements

My parents, my siblings, my extended family of uncles and aunts, grandparents, cousins, and everyone else who just adopted my family as their own.

To my children, Peri, Elric, and Dante. And their mother, Jan.

To my former editors and co-conspirators; Jan Innes, L.B. Wielenga, M.K. Brake, Mariya Andriichuk, Ophidian, Daniel McTaggart, Hannah Migliore, Barbara Holmes, Mike Guttierrez-May, Jessica Lorraine Zickefoose, Aysha Nasser, Larry Jaffe, and countless others who contributed to what you see before you. To Mary Tomasky, who contributed in many ways. To Mrs. Rowe, who got me to write my first poem. And to the Suicide Girls, whose citation of me on Twitter drew attention to my words and works. To the Catholic schoolgirl in the first row (yes, I saw your Sharon Stone impression).

To those who have inspired me, empowered me, and raised me from the dead more times than I can count. To my teachers, ministers, and friends along the road. To those who fell, those who wounded me, those who healed me, those who taught me, those who fought me, and those who endured.

To those whose names I cannot name because they have their own shadows to hide within and/or the muses who have never granted me the grace that I have granted them. I understand when I can and accept when I cannot. Immortality is a hard mantle to wear. We need for small gods in this graceless age.

www.ingramcontent.com/pod-product-compliance
Lightning Source LLC
Chambersburg PA
CBHW051406070526
44584CB00023B/3319